I am so glad Bill wrote this book. It's a way of putting his heart on paper and making it available to the whole Body of Christ worldwide. My hope is that through this book many others will have the same life-changing experience that we have had. I strongly recommend this book as a practical manual that comes from a man who really knows what spiritual mentorship is. Don't expect vague theories; this is not Bill's way at all. On the contrary, his life will come out on these pages. Bill and Laurie mentor with commitment, sacrifice, and love.

Jorge Carvalho
OC/Sepal Director in Romania

This book is long overdue, but then again, it's been a lifetime in the making. I believe it will be used as a guidebook for many as they seek to carry out the exhortation of 2 Timothy 2:2.

Phil Comer
Author, Co-founder Intentional Parents International
Founding Pastor, Westside: A Jesus Church
Portland, Oregon

Course of a Mentor

Empowering Protégés to

Fulfill Their God-given Potential

By Bill and Laurie Keyes

Course of a Mentor: Empowering Protégés to Fulfill
Their God-Given Potential

Edited by Rachael Grotte.
Cover by Tony Sorci.

Published by Missional Challenge Publishing.
www.missionalchallenge.com

Manufactured in the U.S.A.

ISBN: 978-1-939921-92-5

Dedication

We dedicate this book to our family who've sacrificed, challenged and encouraged us over these 55 plus years to accomplish all that God had desired of us.

Contents

Part 3: Pressing On

Foreword

Ten years ago, Bill and Laurie Keyes saved my marriage.

My wife and I married at 21 and church planted at 23.

Exactly.

Seven years in, the church plant was going quite well, but our marriage was falling apart. Honestly, it was tough from day one. We are very different personalities, from very different families of origin, with very different ideas about what life together could look like. Combine that with the idealism of our culture around marriage and romance, and we were in a bad way.

Seven years in, I was also still trying to change my wife to fit my ego ideal, rather than coming to delight in her soul as a gift in my life. She was working on me from the other direction.

We needed help, or we were going to end up out of church leadership, and fast. We knew the Keyes through my parents, who raved about them as mentors, and decided they were our best hope for a safe place to get help.

A short plane ride to Colorado, and we were sitting in their home, in tears, learning truths and practices that would radically alter the trajectory of our marriage. They spent two long days with us. Never charged us a penny. Never asked anything in return. I think they even paid for our meals. They just gave, with radical generosity, of their time, wisdom, and love.

This book is yet another example of their generosity. The wisdom in these pages will cement their legacy as mentors and leaders. The time has come for us to take the baton, and love those coming up behind us the way we have been loved.

John Mark Comer
Author of *Loveology* and
The Ruthless Elimination of Hurry
Pastor of Vision & Teaching
Bridgetown Church, Portland, OR

Preface

Hello there! My name is Darlene Dueck. I am the third daughter of Bill and Laurie Keyes, born into their home in 1967. Today, I am a mother of four adult children.

When Dad asked me to write a preface for their book on mentoring, my first response was, "Absolutely! I have watched you and mom live out a life of mentoring from as early as I can remember." This is true; there has never been a time in my life that I do not remember coming home to a living room of either women, young men, or couples who were spending intentional and quality time with my parents. Throughout my most formative years, I was impressed with the value that both Dad and Mom placed on people.

It is no wonder Dad decided to put into words what he has been living out for most of his days. I have seen his commitment to mentoring first-hand. I have heard the words of affirmation and appreciation from those they have been mentoring. It is real. Both Mom and Dad have truly taken on a lifestyle of investing in relationships.

However, there was a key moment not too long ago that stands out indelibly in my mind. Fall of 2011. Dad and Mom were six months into their second commitment to Brazil residency. They had been asked to move to Brazil to be strategic in mentoring the Brazil/Sepal team. I thought this idea was amazing and I admired the way they were so willing to invest deeply by moving to be near the people they were mentoring. But this was also the fall when my oldest son was entering college. As he was a collegiate athlete, my husband and I became more aware that there would need to be some adjustment to our schedules in order to actively be present at his games. As for our three other children, each one was in a unique stage in life (middle school and high school) that was beginning to take more and more intentional time out of our schedules.

The phone conversation started like this, "Hey Dad! How's it going? What are you and Mom up to this weekend?" His response was a strategic gift to me. They were having unexpected visa problems. We continued with the regular run down of what my kids were up to and what I had going on with classes coming up that fall. I was teaching at our local middle school and always loved my conversations with Dad over what I was currently teaching in World History.

Soon, the conversation turned. "Dad, there's something on my heart to tell you...(pause)...I am feeling like I just need to say, IT'S TIME." I know that comment went far deeper than just Dad's ears. His heart heard this and later I would find out that it was my comment that started both Mom and Dad on a path to return back to the United States. It would set them on a path of soon relocating to Colorado, into partial retirement, and then to the Bay Area where they would live for the next four years. Later Dad would say to me, "Mom and I decided to live in California in order to be within driving distance of any/all of our kids and grandkids." That was intentionality first-hand.

Preface

Since then, I have had the privilege of once again sitting in the front row as I have watched Dad (and Mom) live out intentional mentoring with my three siblings and the 14 grandkids they so deeply care about and actively mentor. Even in my personal experience, there have been times when my husband and I have been in needy moments wanting advice and input. We too turn to my parents who drop everything and are present. They walked closely with us during our difficult years of unemployment. They mentored us through the years of raising our children into adults. Today, even my own children often say, "I have a phone date with Papa and Nana."

I cannot think of a better example of generational mentoring than what I have witnessed first-hand with my dad and mom. The principles in this book have been genuinely lived out before ever being written out. They lived this, modeled this, and now are passing it on for others to make similar marks on relationships and family.

Darlene Dueck
Daughter of Bill and Laurie

A Word from Bill...

Early one morning, I was awakened from deep sleep and I felt a strong sense from God that I was to write a book. Had I ever before felt a similar challenge? Never!

Different friends and colleagues had mentioned in passing that I should write, but this day was very different!

All at once, I had in my mind the title, the various sections of the book, and even the chapter titles. Never had I sensed so strongly a calling to write. The whole book was before me in my heart and mind.

I immediately got up, and after a cup of coffee and a prayer, I started writing. The message I heard in my heart was: "Bill, look back and see what I have done to bring many people into your life. See how they have been used by Me to mentor you and shape you into becoming who you are today."

Relationships determine the quality of the mentoring process, and the most important relationships in my life have shaped the outcome of my life. The concept of mentoring was being established in me from my youth. My beginnings, looking back, were filled with what I call *spontaneous, unintentional mentoring*. This type of mentoring is birthed out of relationships with people we trust and admire. These impactful relationships were used of God to mentor me in a very broad yet specific way. We are hopeful that as you read my story, this will become apparent.

As I continued to look back, I could see that God had clearly given me a specific mission in life—to help others discover for themselves what God wants of them. The calling I was feeling so strongly that morning was to tell parts of my story in order to reveal God's work in me *through others*, and then share how God has enabled me to do the same *for others*.

There are three parts to this manuscript:

Part I: a recounting of my story and of experiences which reveal God using people to mentor me.

Part II: a focus on mentoring, the main topic of the book, and how it can best be done.

Part III: a challenge to embrace mentoring for your future.

The goal of this book is to see people equipped to touch other people's lives, which then results in the multiplication of changed lives, and the mentoring process continues.

It is amazing to experience the power of a person speaking directly, personally, and with blessing into our lives. One day, Paul Yaggy, an older mentor of mine, put his hand on my shoulder, looked into my eyes, and said: "I see in you the ability to lead and influence others to become Christ's followers." I was never the same after that. It was a breath of life to me. (I recognize this as *spontaneous intentional mentoring*.)

A Word from the Author

Our hope is that this book will breathe greater life and purpose into your soul, and that as a result, you will see and embrace mentoring as a part of your life.

Bill Keyes
(for Laurie too)

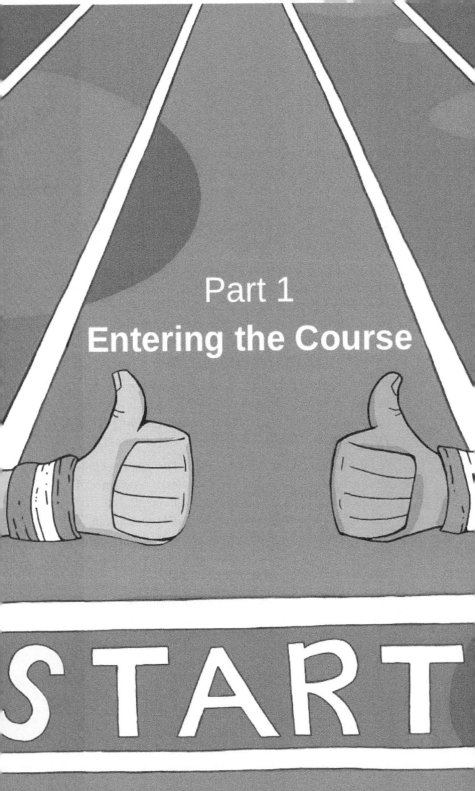

Few people exemplify a lifetime of mentoring as powerfully as Bill and Laurie Keyes. Together they helped recruit my wife Kathie and me into missions with One Challenge over 30 years ago. They challenged us with their lives, walked with us as friends and invested in our development as leaders.

Bill and Laurie inspire us to follow Jesus wholeheartedly and to look toward the horizon of God's purposes for our lives. They believe in us… and what a difference that has made. Their support accelerated our growth, their counsel lifted our trajectory, and their mentoring multiplied influence into the lives of many.

Countless missionaries and leaders serving around the world could share a similar story. The Keyes' investment in others has created a ripple effect now touching over 100 countries. Together, we are part of their legacy.

In this compact book, Bill Keyes shares principles of life-on-life mentoring distilled from decades of experience. As a missionary, marathoner and mountaineer, Bill is known for his ability to focus on a goal, lay out a plan, take others with him and persist to a successful end. His foresight is evident as he gives us practical tools to help people reach their God-given potential.

I know you'll enjoy these pages, and if applied well, you too with leave a legacy in the lives of others.

Dr. Dean Carlson
One Challenge President

Chapter 1
God's Call

In the summer of 1957, when I was 15 years old, I asked my father if I and a friend of mine could borrow his Corvette (1955) to drive to summer camp. He agreed. He let us plan our trip, take his Corvette, and trusted our choices. We were all going to the same Bible camp with plans to meet later that day at a conference center in Big Bear, California, where my mom and dad were directing the program.

Around 9 a.m. that morning, we left the greater Los Angeles area. My buddy, Fred, who was 17 years old, was the driver. No more than 30 minutes into our trip, we suddenly crashed the Corvette, going through the freeway exchange where the Pasadena and Golden State freeways cross. Hitting the oncoming traffic divider, we went over the median and crashed into the chain link fence which prevented us from falling 50 feet into the Los Angeles basin far below. The Corvette was completely totaled. Had it not been primarily for God's protection, our seatbelts and the fact that no car was entering the freeway at that moment, my life could have ended there.

No one was seriously injured, but I went into a medically defined "state of shock." I made a phone call to my dad telling him what had happened. I was expecting to hear some strong and even harsh words from him; after all, we had demolished his sports car that he really enjoyed. Instead, he only expressed concern for me, our physical state, our safety, and his love for us. In that moment, he reflected God's love in a way I will never forget. As I look back on this today, I can see that my theology of a loving, compassionate God was in formation that day. My dad was *spontaneously, unintentionally mentoring* me.

Sometime later we finally made it up to camp, and I spent that first day recovering. I will never forget my mom's words to me, "God must have something very special for you in life, because that is the second time He has saved your life." She went on to say that when she was seven months pregnant with me, she was in a terrible car accident. My dad was driving. They entered an intersection on a green light as another car ran through a red light and hit the door on the driver's side of their car. The impact threw my mother out of the passenger side of the car 15 feet. All her ribs were broken, along with other injuries, but God saved her life and mine. As I listened, I felt the impact of her words, "God must have something very special for you in life." Again, God used another person, my mother, to raise my awareness of His sovereign purpose for my life.

I was beginning to learn of God's Sovereignty. Had I died in either accident, everything that you read in this book would have never happened and my own family would have never been a reality. That is a shocking thought, but again God was using the *spontaneous, unintentional mentoring* of my mom to shape me.

God's amazing, sovereign grace brought me through that experience and today I have a marriage of over 56 years; our four children with their spouses all walk with God; and they have established Christ-centered homes with 14 grandchildren that represent the potential of 14 homes that could do the same. The importance of what God has done in our family will become apparent later as we talk about the Biblical multiplication process in mentoring.

My spiritual life began at the age of nine. My parents were committed Christians. I remember one Sunday, after church, asking my mom to sit with me at the top of the stairs in our Hollywood home on June 29, 1951. There, I opened my heart to Jesus and let him in. My mother used the verse Revelation 3:20, *"Here I am! I stand at the door and knock. If anyone hears my voice and opens the door, I will come in and eat with him and he with me."* After that day, I never doubted my salvation; but at age 15 and a half, after the accident on the way to camp that week, I surrendered my whole life to Christ—past, present and future. I was 100 percent open to whatever God had for me. From that day forward, I prayed and lived for God's will.

During my high school years, I had both teachers and coaches who impacted my life. I experienced this influence through what we now identify as *spontaneous, intentional mentoring*. Jim Dwinell, a youth pastor in our local church, had a significant affect on my life as he helped me to see both God's priorities and my abilities. He also emphasized the Great Commission that Jesus left us in Matthew 28, which caused me to consider missions for my life. One coach in particular, Jim Kliewer, built in me the will to push through adversity and to strive for the best. He also helped me to recognize that my life needed to be committed to God and to others and consistent in order to please both God and man. It was from him that I first learned the principles of "team."

There were several major decisions that I made after that. The first big one that I faced was which college to attend. In high school, I was very involved in student government, leadership, and sports, lettering in three—football, basketball and baseball. During those years, I planned to go to Wheaton College in Wheaton, Illinois, because I wanted to play football there. I applied and was accepted.

At the end of summer, four days before I was to fly to Wheaton for freshman orientation, I woke up very unsettled in my heart about my decision. I had not felt that way before. God was about to intervene in my life once again, and I would learn two major life lessons.

I felt that God himself was mentoring me, using this moment to slow me down, making me pay attention to His will and listen well. I shared how I was feeling with my mom and she simply asked, "Well, if it's not Wheaton, where would you go?" I replied, "I'm not sure mom, but maybe Westmont College." She was shocked and suggested that I call Westmont immediately. Since it was Saturday, no one should have been there to answer the phone that day, but someone was. It was the head of Admissions. In short, he told me that if the next day (Sunday) I could bring him all the information, documents and transcripts that I had shared over the phone, I had a chance to be admitted. I went, and the result was that I started at Westmont one week later with total peace.

The two lessons I learned were: 1) God knows that the commitment of my heart is to follow Him at all costs, and He will redirect my steps knowing what is best for me, and 2) Always make major decisions in prayer, putting God first, pursuing God's direction for your life, taking counsel and listening for His voice above all others.

I knew for certain by December of my freshman year that Westmont College really was the place God had for me. God revealed himself to me in a very personal and supernatural way through the death of my fellow classmate and friend Nancy Voskuyl in a car accident. I was given a deep awareness of the importance of making every day of life count. Suddenly, I was awakened to the seriousness of life.

I graduated in three and a half years with a major in Social Science. My plan was to continue on to school and obtain a Secondary Teaching Credential with the dream of teaching high school, either in the United States or possibly overseas on the mission field.

Again, I experienced *spontaneous, unintentional mentoring* during these years by my college professors and fellow colleagues with whom I lived and studied. I was impacted and consistently challenged to seek God's direction in life. I continued my graduate studies at Los

Angeles State University for one semester, and then God did it again. He redirected my path.

During this time, in April of 1963, I married Laurie Price, my special friend and sweetheart during our high school and college years. At the same time, I was offered the position of youth pastor at our home church, Fountain Avenue Baptist Church in Hollywood, CA. As a youth pastor, I was asked by the church leadership to lead a summer team of young people to Northern California for an evangelistic outreach program called Rural Outreach (a program affiliated with the American Sunday School Union). We went to areas of Northern California where there were no churches. The program was similar to "Five Day Good News Vacation Bible School" programs. God used all of us. We saw God working in ways we had never seen before. With the young people that we trained, a church was planted that summer that continues on today. Praying and seeing the power of prayer in all of our lives impacted us greatly. I knew for sure that I wanted more of what we had just experienced.

Taking time to pray and seeking counsel enabled me to see that God was calling me to work within a church setting rather than in a public high school. It became apparent that I needed to change my course of study and begin theological training as well as studies in the area of Christian Education. God opened the door to attend Talbot Theological Seminary in La Mirada, CA. I completed the master's program of Religious Education (MRE) in two years.

As a young married couple, we were pastoring youth, and for additional income, I was putting in some hours with a messenger service, using my car to deliver packages and mail all over the greater Los Angeles area. During this time, our first child, Donna Laureen, was born.

It was a crazy time, but it was crazy good! We felt God confirming that further training for ministry was critical. This became a much bigger step of faith than we had ever imagined. We thought we would be serving the U.S. church in the role of Director of Christian Education, working with youth in a local church. Then God did it again, changing the direction of our lives.

In 1965, I completed my MRE and waited for God's leading. As we prayed, God began closing doors of opportunity; ten churches contacted us regarding church ministry but nothing concrete happened. Laurie and I were beginning to sense that ministry in the U.S. was not what God had in mind.

We had always been open to missions, but at that point, we began to actively pursue going to the mission field. We examined three agencies in particular. The more we prayed, the more we both felt that Overseas Crusades (OC) matched who we were called to be. OC had the very values and strategies that we were trained in. We saw their heart for both evangelism, discipleship and working "shoulder to shoulder" with nationals.

In addition, their emphasis on family, the importance of working in a team with a focus on discipleship and the principle of multiplication (II Timothy 2:2), along with equipping nationals (Ephesians 4) won our hearts. What we began to see in the lives of Dick Hillis, Bud Schaeffer, Norm Cummings, Tine Hardeman, Luis Palau, and other OC staff impacted us in many ways. We wanted what they had—a real zeal and

7

commitment to serve the Lord with no reservation, come what may.

That summer of 1965, God clearly led, and we made the decision to join Overseas Crusades to become overseas missionaries. They sent us to Farmington, Michigan for nine months to experience a pre-field training program called Missionary Internship.

Again, God continued to stretch us in many ways. By then, our second daughter had been born, Deanne Kathleen. We were studying one week each month with Missionary Internship, and the other three weeks we were serving in a large Presbyterian Church in Pontiac, MI. Since we had been raised in a Baptist Church, by working cross-denominationally God was preparing us to work with the whole Body of Christ. Our focus was to work with youth; however, by working in a larger church, I also had the opportunity to gain experience in many other ministries within that church over the nine-month period. At the end of the training, they wanted us to stay for the summer as well. Our year in Michigan caused our passion for ministry to grow even stronger.

During our training, the founder/president of OC, Dr. Dick Hillis, came and discussed our field assignment and raising support with a faith mission. We will never forget our time with him! We both experienced him as a mentor in our lives—encouraging us in our personal walk with God, our marriage, family and ministry.

This was another period of time when *spontaneous, intentional mentoring* was happening for both of us. When we asked what field he or OC thought would be best for us, without any hesitation, he replied, "Brazil!" He added that in all of OC's other fields (there were seven at that time) the need was primarily for missionaries to work in the field of evangelism. In Brazil, however, effective evangelism was already going on. Their particular need was to strengthen new believers. My passion for Christian Education—deep "precept upon precept" discipleship through churches—specifically met this need. It seemed like a good fit given our education and experience to date. We prayed that God would confirm that to us, and He never led us differently.

After one year of raising support, we were ready to depart for the field, to a country we knew nothing about and to a team we had never met. During that year, our third child, Darlene Shirlayne was born. We were now a family of five—our girls were ages 3, 2, and 3 months. When we were given the green light to depart, we left on a Japanese semi freighter ship from the Port of Los Angeles, ready to spend 28 days out at sea during the summer of 1967 headed to Brazil.

We joined the OC Sepal Brazil team that had begun ministry four years earlier with the encouragement of Billy Graham and an invitation from the Southern Presbyterian Church of Brazil. When we arrived, God had directed several of the original families to new countries of service. We were one of three new families that arrived within a three-month period, and the dynamic of OC's ministry in Brazil was in transition.

Our first objective was language school. It was a nine-month program. I studied in the mornings while Laurie was home with the children, and we switched roles in the afternoons. This worked well as the mission gave household help during those months of studying the Portuguese language, learning the culture and building relationships. We loved the way our mission supported us in our family life and in the process of acculturation.

During a long break from school, God provided an experience that enabled me to learn of His faithfulness in a very difficult, adventurous and sobering way. Let me share it briefly.

In my first year, I participated in a jungle safari with four other missionary men. We took 14 young high schoolers for a week into a very remote area where a Wycliffe family lived among primitive Indians. Our purpose was to share Christ with the eight high schoolers who did not yet know Him and to begin a relationship with each one. I had responsibility for three of the eight. Early on, two of them came to Christ. This coincided with a jeep accident that happened the first night out.

Settled in at our destination on the fifth day, I was in a hammock sharing the Gospel with Chris, the last of the three. As he was listening, a scream suddenly penetrated the air as a huge snake came out of the river bank near us. Everyone went crazy, including us. We all grabbed our .22 rifles and, on one command, shot the snake until it was no more! Obviously, I lost that moment with Chris, and I thought to myself, "Well, this is the second time that I can think of where Satan used a snake to try to detour God's work." However, shortly after that, God brought us another great moment—we returned to our conversation and he accepted Christ that afternoon.

At that very moment, a plane appeared above us. It was a small plane that landed in the middle of the jungle and primitive people. We were curious why it was there.

The pilot had a telegram for "Bill Keyes." The telegram said, "Please return immediately to Sao Paulo. Your wife is in the hospital." Right away, I was concerned because Laurie was pregnant with our fourth child, our first boy. Suddenly nothing was more important to me than to get to her as soon as possible. It was too late for the plane to leave that night, so we departed at dawn the next morning. After two flights and a taxi ride that included running out of gas, I finally arrived in Sao Paulo and went straight to the hospital.

When I got to Laurie, she described what had happened. After leaving church on Sunday night, while walking back to the car in the dark, she fell into an open sewage hole that had been covered with only leaves and debris. Her whole body was in the hole up to her neck. She was helped out and saw a doctor the next day, who checked out her injury and its impact on our unborn child and sent her home.

By Friday, a dangerous staff infection developed in her leg and she passed out at home with our three young girls nearby. Thankfully, a thoughtful neighbor stopped by to check in on our family and he rushed her to the hospital. There was great concern that our baby was at risk and that they might need to amputate her leg. At that point, Laurie, the doctors, our mission team, and friends all wanted me back. So, the plane had come to the jungle to fly me back home.

I am so grateful that Laurie and our baby were safe and that I arrived home quickly to be there with them. After two unsuccessful attempts, the doctors were able to arrest the infection with antibiotics. Within a week, Laurie was recovering at home and continued with a healthy pregnancy. I am also thankful that the Lord had

11

allowed me enough time to lead each of the three young people to Christ. In fact, all eight had received Christ by that time. The subsequent follow-up was amazing as all 14 of these young men were in a weekly Bible study in our home for a year. A lot of *spontaneous, intentional mentoring* went on that year. The majority of them began attending the church we were working in. Today, 50 years later, Chris (the young man who accepted Christ after we killed the snake) is walking with God and serving in his church in Texas.

This first year in Brazil was one of the hardest times of our lives. Language school did not come easily, no matter how hard we labored at it. Other challenges included difficult interpersonal relationships with our OC Sepal Brazil team, loneliness in raising four children in a totally different culture, lack of emotional support from family and friends, and experiencing church in a foreign language. Yet we remained convinced God had called us there, and we were committed to press forward with our OC Brazil mission called SEPAL (Service of Evangelism for Latin America).

As I reflect on our first term in Brazil, four things greatly impacted me:

1) The OC/Sepal team provided incredible support, encouragement and honest accountability. This period became a season of great personal growth. Many of our team members were mentoring these new young missionaries, Bill and Laurie Keyes.

2) After language school, I had the privilege of teaching at the Word of Life Bible School which gave me friendships, mentoring opportunities, ministry partners and opportunities to minister in team throughout Sao

Paulo (the largest city in Brazil). I led a student ministry team each weekend into various local churches with the students I taught during the week. *Spontaneous intentional and spontaneous unintentional mentoring* were a big part of life.

3) God brought a small Bible study group of Brazilian teens to me that gave wonderful opportunities to evangelize and disciple. In that group was a young person who was our office boy at Sepal. His name was Alexandre and he was special to me. He was being raised by a single mom. With him, *spontaneous, intentional mentoring* occurred without me being fully aware of it.

4) In addition, I was asked to assist a small local Presbyterian Church in the south of Sao Paulo, providing help in Christian Education.

I was beginning to learn what ministry was like in a different country and context. How does someone begin with a vision for teaching high school in the United States and end up in South America as a missionary teaching young people in another language the principles of discipleship, evangelism and mentoring? Only God can do that!

Questions for Reflection...

1. As you reflect on how God led Bill and Laurie's journey to Brazil, look back on your own journey. What have been the two or three most impactful moments in your life when you sensed God confirming your life's direction?

2. How did these events impact your life?

3. In your own personal story, how have you experienced *spontaneous intentional* or *spontaneous unintentional mentoring*?

Recently I have been thinking about how Jesus valued people. That thought took me back 47 years to 1972 when Bill Keyes, my professor, asked me to meet with him weekly for a time of mentoring. I was his student at the Word of Life Bible Institute in Atibaia, Sao Paulo, Brazil. At that time, I thought, "Who am I that he would want to meet with me?" It meant so much.

He valued me—and his influence and encouragement continue until today as I serve as the Senior Pastor of the Baptist Church of Morumbi in Sao Paulo, Brazil. I will always be grateful to God for Bill's life. I hope to be able to do with many what he did for me.

May God continue to bless and enable Bill and Laurie to touch many lives. I write this to you, Bill, many years later, realizing that only in heaven will you discover the impact you had on many others.

Lisanias Moura
Friend, Pastor of Morumbi Baptist Church
Sao Paulo, Brazil

Chapter 2
God's Timing

Shortly after arriving in Brazil, I was approached by several missionaries and nationals who asked if I could help them. While at Talbot seminary, I had written my master's thesis on the topic: "The Comparison of Subject Content between Gospel Light Sunday School Curriculum and David C. Cook Sunday School Curriculum." My purpose had been to explore the content, sequence and doctrinal emphasis in the curriculum for children in grades 1-12 (ages 5-17) during their twelve years of Sunday School. Needless to say, I had come to understand both curriculums in depth.

The Committee in Brazil had just finished a major project, translating and culturally adapting the entire Gospel Light Publications curriculum from pre-school through adult. At that time in Brazil, the Brazilian church had no standard Sunday School curriculum available. This project was the first series of lessons available for teaching children the Bible in local churches distributed across denominational lines. As a result, we saw great opportunities for children and adults to discover God personally.

The church leaders who initially purchased this curriculum had the product in their hands, but they had limited understanding of how to use it. They did not understand the unique tool they had been given to educate their children and youth, offering a real, biblical education in the Word of God. The committee asked me if I could train the Brazilian church how to use this curriculum so that the children, youth and adults could learn the Bible and clearly understand the salvation message of the Gospel.

I was amazed at God's timing and the opportunity given to me. Many churches were open to learning about the concept of a Biblically centered Sunday School. Our OC Sepal Brazil team was fully behind this possibility as were Laurie and I. God was opening a door which fit perfectly with our calling to live out Ephesians 4, "equipping the saints for the work of the ministry."

It was at this time, in the fall of 1969, that God blessed us with our fourth child, a son, Dale Lawrence. He was blessed with dual citizenship, both American and Brazilian, something that God continues to use today in his life as a Christian businessman in Brazil. (He and his family currently live and work in the city of Sao Paulo, the same city where we lived in the 60's and 70's.)

After a short time, I organized the "Department of Educational Services" within Gospel Light (in Portuguese: Edicoes Luz do Evangelho). Our OC Sepal

Brazil team, our friends and counselors, encouraged this partnership with Gospel Light while I maintained my commitment to my team as an OC missionary. This decision led to the writing of a course for teachers called: O Bom Professor (The Good Teacher). Anyone who completed the thirteen-lesson course received a certificate.

At the same time, I introduced to the churches and teachers the Gospel Light materials and the "how to" of teaching the Bible in educating children, youth and adults. We ministered to multiple denominations: Baptists, Presbyterians, Assembly of God, Methodists, Lutherans, Congregational, etc. Over ten years, we established strategic centers in Rio de Janeiro, Belo Horizonte, Sao Paulo, Curitiba and Salvador, with many core groups in each city. There were leaders trained in each city to multiply our ministry and train others to do the same.

Over the next decade, God allowed us to impact over 14,000 Bible teachers and church leaders all over the country. We started a Brazilian Christian Education organization called ALEC (The Association of Leaders in Christian Education). It gradually grew into a national organization with national leadership. We had four nearly full-time Brazilians who traveled with me around the country. Some were students that came out of the Word of Life Bible School where we had ministered in our earlier years. One girl who received our training went to the north of Brazil during the following three years and trained over 4,000 teachers and leaders in her denomination.

God gave us many experiences to train, motivate and mobilize Brazilian teachers throughout all of Brazil. One particular session was on the ministry of the Holy Spirit in teaching. A special memory was when a pastor's wife, after learning of the role of the Holy Spirit, acknowledged that she did not have a personal relationship with Christ, and she accepted Him during that training. This whole ministry was another door God opened, enabling us to live out our calling to II Timothy 2:2 where Paul trained Timothy to train faithful men to train others to make Christ followers.

In 1975, our OC Sepal Brazil Field Director left Brazil, and I was asked to become the next Field Director for our team. The OC Sepal Brazil team encouraged me to take this new leadership role. It was a difficult decision because I was still involved with ALEC; however, God used this time to enable national leaders, who we had intentionally mentored, to take over leadership of ALEC and continue training and mentoring teachers.

In 1978, this transition was complete when ALEC as an organization was turned over to a national leader, Eucir Feitosa, who had ministered with me for nearly ten years. One of my greatest joys was to see this Brazilian leader, one who was actively serving with me, take the future leadership of ALEC and continue its ministry nationally for many years.

We saw our OC Sepal Brazil team continue to grow— new members were added, both Americans and Brazilians, and the personal demands on my life and leadership were ever greater. However, God clearly gave me the will and the ability to provide leadership for this growing OC Sepal Brazil team. (*"... for it is God who works in you, both to will and to work for his good pleasure."* Philippians 2:13)

God's Timing

I continued as the Field Director until 1979 when we left for our predetermined furlough-home assignment. We rented out our home in Sao Paulo, stored most of our personal belongings in one of the rooms of our house, and left with plans to be in the States for one year. I did not know at that moment that God was about to move us once again—a further calling within His plan in the bigger picture of life.

Questions for Reflection...

1. Who are the people that have had the biggest impact on your life?

2. How has each one made a difference? Explain.

Chapter 3
God's Redirection

We left Brazil for our "home leave" in June 1979 (returning to the United States), fully expecting to return to Brazil in one year. Soon after we arrived back in the U.S., the leadership of OC asked that we come to its headquarters in Santa Clara, CA, for a debriefing. We were living in Panorama City in Southern California as missionaries in residence with Grace Community Church where Dr. John MacArthur was our pastor. Our children were enrolled in a nearby Christian school and were settled in for the coming year. Our goal was to give our children time to get to know their "roots" with family and country.

The "debriefing" with the OC Leadership Team focused on our lives and ministry in Brazil over the previous four-year term, and acknowledgement of all that God had done: thousands had been trained; many had come to Jesus and been discipled; and some had been intentionally mentored to carry on in our place.

The debrief was an all-day affair. During the morning, we shared the past, present and future plans for Brazil. We received much affirmation. Lunch time came, and we went out to eat with some staff, not knowing that the leadership team continued to meet without us. Once back, we were invited to continue our discussion. We had no idea that God was about to speak to us in a life-changing way once again. It would be the biggest and hardest moment in our life as a couple, as a family and as individuals to date.

The OC Leadership Team listened carefully as we shared our new calling to return to Brazil to help awaken the Brazilian Church toward global missions— our new vision from the Lord, impacted by II Kings 4:1-7. They collectively affirmed this calling for our lives. The turning point in our conversation was the application of all we had shared. They heard our passion for training new Brazilian missionaries for global missions; however, they felt that God could be calling us to remain in the United States to recruit and deploy Americans to Asia, Africa, South America and Europe. At that moment, OC had 107 missionaries in seven overseas countries. The focus of mission mobilization was the same, but the context was very different. They were asking us to leave Brazil, to remain in the States and join the OC leadership team to recruit missionaries from America for missions world-wide.

Our hearts were in Brazil. The pull within our whole family was to live in Brazil. However, we agreed to pray about this new challenge. To help make this decision, we believed that we needed counsel from those that knew us best—the OC Sepal Brazil team. I asked OC leadership for their blessing to return to Brazil in July to seek my team's counsel. This decision was one that we believed would be best made in team. I returned alone to Sao Paulo, Brazil. The cost for all six of us to go was too much, which was very hard on all. I spent a week with the OC Sepal Brazil team (those men and women who knew us best) to hear from them and from God through them.

At the end of seven days with our team, their words were clear. They had two responses for our family: 1) emotionally, they did not want us to leave Brazil. Their desire was for us as a family to return and continue with them in Brazil. They wanted us back. Yet they also believed that, 2) God could be leading us to stay in the US to help OC. They saw how my skills as a mobilizer could be useful to recruit missionaries.

With this answer, I left Sao Paulo and returned to my family in Southern California with the team's blessing and the freedom to follow God however He would lead. Honestly, I wanted something more defined. I gathered my family together and shared the team's response with them. I told them, "The decision lies with us." Our children wanted to hear either a "yes" or "no," and they eagerly hoped for a "yes" to return to Brazil, as did Laurie and I.

For weeks we prayed over this decision together. We strongly believed that we needed to do this together. Each time I asked our children how they felt, they responded, "We want to go home to Brazil." This was the only home they had ever known.

Increasingly God was strengthening my heart for this new role with OC. Emotionally I wanted to return to Brazil, but God was saying to me, "Stay here and lead OC to recruit missionaries for Brazil and the rest of the world." There was much heartache, tears, praying and discussion among our family. I started to feel strongly that God was leading us to stay. I felt that God led me to ask Laurie and our children the question, "If God is asking us to make this move, can you trust me and say 'yes'?" There was reluctant agreement.

Our decision was to stay in the U.S., trusting together that this was God's redirection. This decision was made in November 1979. It was the "death" of a vision and it hurt. However, God's provisions for us were amazing grace! To recall them all would fill another book, but we need to name a few: emotional freedom to move away from friends and family in Southern California, new friends in Northern California, a church with a youth group that was reaching young people for Jesus, and a fully furnished home for us when we had literally no savings in our bank account.

We started with OC in Santa Clara, CA., on February 1, 1980. Little did we know that the experience of the next 30 years would be of value to our beloved Brazilians in 2010.

Questions for Reflection...

1. In your life, what have been defining moments where God has redirected you? How have they affected your life, relationships and direction?

2. How did you question or have that decision affirmed afterward? How do you feel about it today?

3. If you have experienced the "death" of a vision, explain. What is the value it holds for you today?

Chapter 4
God's Faithfulness to
Lead and Guide

After 13 years of having had a national ministry, field leadership, training leaders throughout Brazil, teaching in several seminaries and Bible schools in a country the size of the U.S. plus another Texas, I suddenly found myself starting all over again. I had an empty office, one part-time secretary, and a 3x5 metal box with cards representing approximately 40 names of recruiting contacts that OC had at that moment. That was literally where and how I began in my new role as Director of Recruitment.

Only God knew what was ahead for us. I see now that all of what happened was clearly from Him! This new chapter in our lives became another God story. In 30 years, from 1980 when we began this new ministry to 2010, OC grew from 107 missionaries to nearly 250 missionaries including nationals and staff personnel, serving in 27 countries.

I grew too, learning and being mentored by godly men with whom I served. At the beginning, my role was Director of Recruitment, but after a time, the OC Leadership Team asked that I assume the role of Vice President of Personnel. My team of 1.5 persons grew to over a dozen. It was an amazing team with very gifted and experienced cross-cultural missionaries that had returned to the States similarly to me, to take on a new ministry different from their field experience. God blessed me and OC with this team.

Our personal awareness of needs on the mission field enabled us, with God's wisdom, to develop individual departments for Recruitment, Training, Member-care, Leadership Development, and Personnel Development. We were also able to develop special programs for the training of missionary kids. Our own children joined us in leading and developing the training programs for these children and youth. God had all of this in mind during our years of intense service in Brazil.

There were special opportunities for ministry that came to me during those years as well. I had the privilege of connecting with and recruiting from many theological seminaries and Bible schools (i.e. Talbot Theological Seminary, Dallas Theological Seminary, Gordon Conwell Theological Seminary, Fuller Theological Seminary and Regents University in Canada, to name a few). In addition, we partnered with the Association of Church Mission Committees (ACMC) and assisted various local churches in the development of their mission programs. All of this was clearly in line with our original calling to II Timothy 2:2 and Ephesians 4. We will forever be full of gratitude to our supporters and supporting churches who stayed committed to us and the ministry God had called us to. Today, 50+ years later, many of them are still on our team.

Involvement in the local manifestation of the Body of Christ has always been a major commitment of ours. Biblically, the Church is the institution established by God to carry out the Great Commission that Jesus left us with in Matthew 28:18-20 when He said, "Go into all the world..." Mission agencies are instruments that assist and help the church do that task world-wide. Wonderful mentoring from experienced missionaries greatly prepares the young people who are being called to take strong steps toward career field service.

During our first ten years, my wife and I also assisted in the mission program of our home church in San Jose, CA. Over 100 young people and adults participated in a monthly missions training program with regular mentoring and assessments. About twenty percent of them were deployed into full-time missionary service, and the rest became people who prayed and gave financially more knowledgeably.

Our ministry with OC in Brazil as well as in the states focused on discipleship, servanthood, multiplication, family, partnerships, team, and creativity—all for the strengthening of the Body of Christ. Each of these areas of focus became values of OC over time as orchestrated by God through the leadership of OC.

We worked in teams both in the U.S. and globally. Over the years, I have had the privilege of serving in leadership with five of OC's presidents: Dr. Clyde Cook,

Rev. Paul Yaggy, Dr. Larry Keyes, Dr. Greg Gripentrog and Dr. Dean Carlson.

The more I have served others, the more I have sensed that God was using me to influence and to help them discover for themselves what God wanted for their lives—this is the ministry of mentoring. I have experienced God's pleasure as I have watched lives change with a greater awareness of both God's purposes for them and the realization of those purposes being for God's glory.

What I found myself doing more and more was a form of mentorship without even knowing it. Laurie and I spent hours with couples and individuals, visiting them, spending time in their homes, inviting them into our home, training and counseling them. Now, years down the road, we have heard from several of these people who have given us glimpses of the impact of the mentoring that took place. Additionally, we can now see that God was working in and through us in preparation for something that He had in His future plan for us. This discovery was building toward the "apex" of our lives and ministry.

Questions for Reflection...

1. What are some of the opportunities and/or open doors that God has given you in the past to impact others? Explain.

2. How have those relationships affected where you are today?

I remember very well the impact the SEPAL missionaries had on the Brazilian pastors and leaders when they arrived in Brazil during the 70s. I was one of those young pastors who was greatly blessed by their lives.

What I could have never foreseen, nor dreamed, was something that happened some years later. In 2010, I reconnected with Bill Keyes, one of those missionaries that served in Brazil in the 60s and 70s. My wife, Sirley, and I were receiving some specialized training at OC's International Headquarters in Colorado. Shortly before we returned to Brazil, God prompted me to ask Bill a question. I asked, "Bill, would you and Laurie be open to return to Brazil once again, this time to help me in the areas of recruitment, training and deploying new Sepal missionaries?" Bill's eyes opened wide with excitement. Sometime later, Bill and Laurie were living just two blocks from our apartment and that relationship has continued until today.

Bill has been my mentor, someone in whom I can confide, share my dreams, thoughts, doubts and fears. During the past 10 years, our relationship has come to the point of really missing each other when we are not able to Skype or see each other.

Bill has left an indelible mark on my life through the commitment he has toward me. Our prayers for each other have enabled us together to serve many leaders and their churches so that God's mission may be realized throughout the world. May God be praised for the lives of Bill and Laurie Keyes.

Oswaldo Prado
Friend, Missionary with Sepal/Brazil
Pastor, Author

Chapter 5
God's Call is for Everyone

From the beginning, when we joined OC in 1965, it has been my privilege to work with, serve and learn from many godly, gifted men and women both in Brazil and the U.S. These include American teammates: Jim and Judy Kemp, Hans and Alice Wilhelm, Paul and Carol Landry, Paul and Joanne McKaughan, Larry and Shirley Keyes, John and Carolyn Quam, Joe and Diane Walsh, Jim and Julie McNutt, Tim and Lois Halls, Ken and Diane Kudo, Harmon and Carol Johnson, and Doug and Joyce Spurlock. Many Brazilian leaders joined with us: Ary and Carolyn Velloso, Paulo Moreira, Sulamita Ferreira, Tereza Ichiki, Eucir and Neide Feitosa, and many more who impacted me deeply. Likewise, in the U.S., men such as Dr. Dick Hillis, Dr. Luis Palau, Dr. Clyde Cook, Rev. Paul Yaggy, Rev. Norm Cummings, Dr. John MacArthur, Dr. Greg Gripentrog and others were used of God to help shape my heart and soul. They have each contributed to who I am today. I mention this as a powerful illustration of "life on life"—when one life influences another as one disciples, coaches, or mentors.

In retrospect, I have had people influencing me at every stage of my life. Often in our lives God brings a community of people to us who build uniquely into us. My life path has taken me into many different areas of life: academia, sports, music, ministry, a cross-cultural world, etc. In each one, I have been influenced by individuals who have stopped to speak into my life and some that have walked with me during part of my journey. I see how I have been impacted by both *spontaneous intentional* and *spontaneous unintentional mentoring*. You never know when God may use you to touch a life in a significant way. We need to always be on the alert and prepared to invest in others.

Let me share two stories that have been particularly significant in my life.

First, in 2010 Laurie and I had been asked by both OC and Sepal to return to Brazil for one year to assist our Sepal team. In May of that year, we participated in Sepal's annual Leadership Conference for pastors and leaders. Just before the opening session, Laurie and I were helping to welcome attendees from all over Brazil (approximately 1,700 participants), when a man named Alexandre approached me. (Do you remember the young teen in chapter one, our OC Sepal Brazil office boy, who, along with his buddies, participated in a weekly Bible Study with me? It was him all grown up!) He asked, "Do you remember me?" And immediately I said, "YES!" I recognized him after nearly 30 years. After a short, very exciting conversation, he excused himself and went up to the platform. You never know what God may be doing when you are investing into a person's life. Alexandre became a leading pastor in Brazil, and on that night, he was one of two opening speakers in that Sepal Leadership Conference. What a delightful surprise!

Second, after seven months living in Brazil, we were spending part of a day with Jorge and Virginia Carvalho, whom we had invested time into during their pre-field missionary training. During our lunch at the food court in a shopping mall, Jorge grabbed my hand and said, "I want to ask you a question, and before I ask it, I need you to say 'yes'." After a brief moment, because I trusted him and sensing the spirit of the moment, I said "yes." Then he asked me, "Will you make a commitment to mentor us when we go to Romania as Sepal missionaries?" Having already said yes, now with full understanding, I affirmed my "yes." That "yes" was the beginning of our commitment to Jorge and Virginia and, from that time until now, to mentoring Sepal Brazil missionaries all over the world.

Today we are mentoring many Brazilian missionary couples. There have been others as well that we have mentored over the years from other mission agencies, as well as U.S. pastors and their wives. In the ensuing chapters, I will explain what this commitment to mentoring represents. It is one of the most rewarding and fulfilling ministries we have had.

I realize now, in an even greater way, that this is what Christ did with His disciples. He mentored them. And this is what He wants of us as we work with and personally relate to those He brings into our lives. Mentoring is "life on life" over time.

Since my decision at age 15 to surrender my life fully to the will of God, I have asked Him many times to enable me to fulfill His purposes. We all run the race of life personally. We are challenged to run hard and to finish "the race" which He has prepared for us. Today, at age 77, both Laurie and I thank God that He continues to bless us with strength and energy to go on, both nationally and internationally, with this purpose. We continue asking for His blessing and strength to run as He enables us.

God has brought specific men and women into our lives. It is our privilege now to mentor and encourage others in their personal growth. We see everyone as unique, special and gifted to serve both God and man. Each person has been given gifts, abilities, talents, and experiences, not as ends in themselves, but as God would have them used.

Accepting the commitment to mentor needs to be a priority. It requires prayer, time, flexibility, availability, and discipline. Mentoring is a challenge that most people can consider. The number of people you can mentor may vary greatly from time to time and it may also depend upon the interest, readiness, and availability of others. God will make that clear in every situation.

It is our joy to journey alongside those that God gives to us and we commit to mentor intentionally. We simply follow the example Christ gave as He worked and lived with His disciples. In the following chapters, there is a more direct focus on mentoring and its impact on both Laurie and me.

Questions for Reflection...

1. Think of the names of people that you have been able to impact in some way.

2. Reflect on how your relationship with them started and what the outcome has been.

3. Reflect on the strength of those relationships.

4. After reading this chapter, who is it that God has put on your heart to mentor?

Part 2
Equipped to
Train Others

A Special Acknowledgement

Recently we have experienced a strong reminder of God's sovereignty. In following through on God's calling to write this book on mentoring, we made a stunning discovery. What God, by His Spirit, has led us to think, live and practice in our mentoring, has also been a part of Bobb Biehl's life and ministry. We have experienced this same reality globally over the years in missions—passions birthed by the Spirit of God are being lived out in ministry very similarly in different parts of the world.

We have enjoyed connecting with Bobb about this; his ready response on the phone is always, "How can I help you?" As he expresses concepts and principles in his writings so similar to our own, he has given his permission to use some of his titles and thoughts—which we have intermingled with our own in Part 2: Equipped to Train Others. Chapters 6-12 are a reflection of our joint passions, ideas and words. (In some cases, we have taken Bobb's very words which are referenced in the Notes at the end of the book.)

We want to thank Bobb, who contributed so much to this project. We would also like to recommend that you pursue his materials at BobbBiehl.com. His recent books are: *Sharing Your Faith* and *Decade by Decade*.

One who makes tapestries is an artist who works day after day on his loom, creating colors and patterns on beautiful fabrics. Throughout my life, God has given me individuals who have weaved a similar work into my life that has caused me to grow and be more fruitful.

The Lord has given me partners with different gifts that enable me to advance and grow in my life. Sometimes this input is more consistent, other times less, but the sharing of ideas, Biblical truths, and life experiences, all with a heart to help and confront, is so helpful.

I am grateful for the lives of Bill and Laurie Keyes who have been mentors and partners with us in our journey as missionaries in Portugal during this past decade. My wife and I have been helped to grow and further conform to the image of Christ.

Rubens Luz
Friend, Missionary/field director to Portugal with Sepal/Brazil

Chapter 6
Intentional Mentoring

"Can you think of three people in your life that have most helped you to become the person you are today?" I was 22 years old when I was first asked that question. As you can see in the first five chapters of this book, my response came easily. God used a youth pastor, an athletic coach, a seminary professor and a missionary statesman to shape my life. Various spiritual and physical qualities were lived out before me through those men. God brought others into my life later who did the same. During my years in Brazil serving as a missionary with OC, God used team members and nationals to further impact my personal growth and ministry. These were definite years of being mentored for me, and I have passed on to others what they invested in me.

While serving in Brazil, our emphasis of ministry was discipleship, evangelism and leadership development. In 1980, after returning to the U.S., God continued to bring opportunities for mentoring into my life. However, while I sensed that my impact was broadening, it was not necessarily deepening. God brought this forcibly to my attention when I asked myself this question:

"If I were to suddenly be removed from all this ministry, what would I be leaving behind? Am I leaving a legacy that He would be pleased with?"

God revealed to me then the difference between my ministry of discipleship/leadership training and my ministry of mentorship. What I saw in Scripture in a new way was how mentoring was actually a model of ministry. I saw this in the life of Barnabas as he came alongside Saul and walked with him.

An Old Testament example of mentorship can be seen in the relationship between Moses and Joshua. John Maxwell describes it this way:

> Not long after the children of Israel escaped from Egypt, Moses selected Joshua to be his assistant. He was described as one of Moses' 'choice men" (Num. 11:28 NKJV). Wherever Moses went, Joshua went with him, whether it was to go up Mount Sinai or to meet with God in the tabernacle, after the Hebrews refused to enter the promised land, the mentoring relationship between the two men continued. The process lasted forty years and culminated with Moses imparting his authority to the younger man. We read in Deuteronomy 31:7 (NKJV): "Then Moses called Joshua and said to him in the sight of all Israel, 'Be strong and of

good courage, for you must go with this people to the land which the Lord has sworn to their fathers to give them, and you shall cause them to inherit it.'"[1]

This kind of mentoring involves a full commitment of one person to another. It can be for a short period or a long time, but it is always based on relationship. My personal discovery was that I had always focused on content and passing on knowledge to those I trained. The difference between my role as a trainer and my role as a mentor was the added component of developing a deep relationship with those whom I mentor.

This discovery resulted in a major shift in my thinking regarding the significance of mentoring relationships. I could now see how mentorship calls for a deeper relationship with someone you enjoy, believe in, and want to see fully develop in life and ministry. When I mentor an individual, there is a bond of hearts, a commitment of care and support, mutual encouragement and security. Every mentoring relationship is different, but most will have these elements. This takes time and requires availability. Christ exemplified this as He spent time with His disciples.

There will be unique differences with each protégé to whom you commit. They will have different personalities, strengths, abilities, gifting, weaknesses, desires, availability, etc. This awareness requires you to respond to each one differently.

The longer you mentor someone, the more you know and understand one another mutually. It is interesting that over time, your mentoring relationship can move to more of a friendship, and then possibly a mutual mentoring begins. This is a very enjoyable level of relationship to experience.

Oswaldo Prado is someone who exemplifies a mutual relationship. Our relationship began 12 years ago when he spent several weeks in our home. He requested mentoring to learn how to better lead as Director of Recruitment for Sepal Brazil, something that I had done for nearly 30 years with One Challenge. Over the years, our relationship grew from mentor and protégé to us mentoring each other. We both have experiences and skills that we share to strengthen each other in life and ministry. Most recently, we challenged and cautioned each other regarding our intense paces of life and ministry. What a blessing.

Once you have an understanding of mentoring, you can begin. A mentoring relationship can start as simply as any other relationship does. As you spend time together, you may naturally begin touching some or all of the following areas:

- Family and marriage

- Finances

- Personal growth

- Career issues

We have challenged most of those whom we have mentored to think about Luke 2:52, "And Jesus grew in wisdom, and stature, and in favor with God and men." We see in this verse the additional areas of:

- Spiritual

- Mental

- Emotional

- Social

- Physical

(Note: We also used this when considering the development of our own children.)

Part of the role of a mentor is to help your protégé work through these areas and others, identifying issues, praying through problems, working through difficulties—always moving them forward toward greater maturity in Christ and in life.

Mentors are those who have gone before on the path of life. They see someone, pause and extend a hand to help them along the way, and/or they extend a safety line of love and affirmation that may keep someone from falling. The mentoring relationship happens when the mentor turns to the protégé and says, "I believe in you, I want to help you succeed." As the mentors, we make our experiences and resources available in any way we can so that they can become all that God wants them to be.

Over the years, my wife and I have addressed many different concerns with our protégés. Here is a list of issues, in no particular order. It is not exhaustive, but it represents the type of conversations that we have experienced:

- the raising and disciplining of children

- raising funds and money management

- dealing with field leadership issues

Course of a Mentor

- cultural and linguistic adjustments
- commitment and its implications
- education of children when living overseas
- setting goals and priorities
- awareness of personal values
- understanding and honoring the Sabbath
- dealing with failure
- submission to authority
- marital difficulties
- aging parents
- retirement
- further education
- personal disciplines
- team-life and struggles
- sickness/death
- conflict with nationals
- understanding the value of differing personalities
- theological differences
- conflict with teammates
- accountability
- lack of communication

For each situation, God gives us grace, wisdom and understanding. Laurie and I ask the Lord each time we are mentoring that He give us discernment and "promptings" by His Spirit so that we move with Him in our conversations. For us, this is the key to understanding ourselves and others. So often, He surprises us with what He has done in and through us. Mentoring is a life of adventure.

Questions for Reflection...

1. Reflecting on the names that you mentioned in chapter 5, what have you considered significant in your times with them?

2. What might you do to make those relationships even stronger?

3. What are some of the topics that you have addressed in your mentoring of them?

For more than 30 years my wife, Diane, and I have gone to Bill and Laurie Keyes when we needed mentoring and guidance. They have a unique, God-given ability and anointing to speak into situations in a way that brings clarity into our confusion. Their winsomeness and wisdom have brought us biblical hope and practical help time and time again when we didn't know what to do or which way to go. And I am not alone! Hundreds of missionaries, pastors, and couples have been helped in much the same way as Bill and Laurie have helped us.

Phil Comer
*Author, Co-founder Intentional Parents International
Founding Pastor, Westside: A Jesus Church
Portland, Oregon*

Bill Keyes has mentored hundreds of men, missionaries, and ministry leaders over the last several decades. He and Laurie have poured themselves into our church staff, enabling us to understand how to function as a team, as well as where each of us fit on the team. In Bill's upbeat, hope-filled way, he can't help but clap his hands in glee when he sees the "ah-ha!" moment light up our faces.

But really, what we have learned from Bill and Laurie is mostly personal—for us and for our family. They have guided us into becoming spiritually, relationally, and emotionally healthy people. Phil and I will be forever grateful for the help and guidance— the mentoring— Bill and Laurie have given us.

Diane Comer
*Friend, Pastor's wife, Author
Co-founder Intentional Parenting International*

Chapter 7
What Mentoring IS NOT

Mentoring has some very distinguishing characteristics. At times it can be misrepresented or labeled something else, other than what it really is. It is important to clearly define what mentoring is; however, I will begin by specifically clarifying what it is not.

Mentoring is *not* evangelism, nor is it discipleship.

Mentoring is *not* an apprentice, nor a coaching relationship.

Mentoring is *not* based on simply matching two people together.

We all need to be involved in evangelism and discipleship. I am very committed to both. I believe that one of the easiest misunderstandings is that mentoring is just another word for discipleship. So, let me repeat: **mentoring is not discipleship**.

This chart, developed by Bobb Biehl is helpful to me in perceiving the differences between evangelism, discipleship and mentoring. Seeing these distinctions will aid in identifying one's calling to ministry. Keep in mind your spiritual gifting and/or personality.

	Evangelism	Discipleship	Mentoring
Is it Scriptural?	Taught and modeled in Scripture	Taught and modeled in Scripture	Modeled in Scripture
Models in Scripture…	Paul	Timothy	Barnabas
Degree of Need?	Desperate	Desperate	Desperate
Primary basis of interchange	Content	Content	Relationship
Type of Role:	Reasoning with non-believers and defending the faith: Presenting the Good News	Teaching new believers scriptural truths. The basics of the Christian Life.	Caring for and helping a person in all aspects of life.
Who's agenda?	Evangelist's agenda (the gospel) helping people see and understand the Gospel.	Discipler's agenda (spiritual disciplines). Learning how to be a Christ follower.	Protégé's agenda (dreams and goals/ problems).[1]

Modeling is a big part of mentoring, but modeling in itself is not mentoring. The primary difference is that a mentor is personally aware of the protégé and wants to use his/her resources to help the protégé reach their God-given potential. Therefore, spending time together in discussions and engaging conversations is very important to the mentoring process. This is a key aspect of mentoring.

As we focus on what mentoring is not and review the chart, let's look now at five common misconceptions about mentoring.

Misconception Number 1: Mentors need to be at least in their 60's (or at least old!).

God can use someone that has many years of experience in life and ministry, but God can equally use a mature sixteen-year-old who understands mentoring and is willing to take the time to commit to younger students who want mentoring. Another example is parents of teens mentoring parents of newborns or couples without children.

Normally, younger protégés look for older "young people" or adults to be their mentors, while mentors normally look for protégés who are younger than they are.

However, Laurie recalls how one of her protégés was effectively mentoring a protégé much older than her. The older woman was new to faith and Laurie's protégé had walked with God deeply for 25 years.

Misconception Number 2: Mentors must be perfect.

This misconception causes qualified people to have misgivings about becoming mentors. The reality is that protégés never actually expect a mentor to be perfect. The best mentors are also teachable people themselves. The following words and phrases have been used to describe mentors:

- *Consistent, stable*

- *Affirming*

- *Believed in me*

- *Accepted me where I was*

- *Saw me as a person of value*

- *Included me in their life*

- *Fun*

- *A person of character, trustworthy*

- *I admired the mentor*

- *There was a naturally positive relationship between us*

- *Knowledgeable and very wise*

What protégés are really concerned about is whether their mentor cares for them and wants to see them succeed in life. You don't have to be 100 percent correct in everything you say. However, you do have to care and be there as much as possible when your protégé has needs, or simply wants to spend time with you.

Misconception Number 3: Mentors have all the answers.

No one has all the answers, and no mentor will ever have all the answers. The mentor's role is to have the answer sometimes, and/or perhaps try and find the answer. (If they do not have the answer, they will seek out where to find it.)

Fundamentally, a mentor tries to connect his/her protégé to the right resources: books, videos, podcasts, articles, e-mail lists, networks, seminars, people, etc. Networking is a real support line for people who mentor others. If a mentor does not have a specific resource, they often know someone else who may lead to the information that is needed.

Misconception Number 4: The mentoring process involves a curriculum that the mentor needs to teach their protégé.

First of all, no such curriculum exists, or if it does, I know nothing of it. The mentoring process is unique to each protégé. What a protégé needs to discover is based on their agenda, experience in life, priorities, questions, needs, etc. It is not based on the mentor's preset program. Very often, my expectations regarding time spent with a protégé are far from what we actually end up talking about. (I think this is true about 70 percent of the time.)

When I began mentoring, I would make a list of topics to discuss, only to discover that what I had planned was not on the protégé's agenda. This happens because the protégé is living with felt needs which a mentor cannot always predict. Neither of us can know the direction of our conversation until we start our time together. More often than not, what I have in mind as a possible focus for discussion rarely becomes our conversation.

Misconception Number 5: A mentor's job is to hold a protégé accountable.

There is a natural tendency to want to hold someone accountable, but this is not a healthy focus. Your focus is to be supporting, strengthening, challenging and encouraging your protégé in their life and ministry. Naturally, we want to see our protégé grow into maturity and there will be a sense of accountability in that process, however that is not your focus. Their accountability is not so much to you as their mentor, but rather to God, to their family, their team and to others to whom they relate.[2]

Questions for Reflection...

1. After reading this chapter, where do you see your strengths to be? Evaluate your giftedness and passion for others.

2. How has this chapter helped clarify your understanding of mentoring?

Chapter 8
What Mentoring IS

A definition of any word needs to be clear, precise and understandable. Here is a definition for mentoring that has given us clarity in our intentional mentoring relationships.

"Mentoring is a lifelong relationship in which a mentor helps a protégé reach his or her God-given potential."
– Bobb Biehl

Over our lifetimes, we have experienced mentors who have poured into us and helped shape who we are and how we serve God each day. We also have poured into hundreds of men and women through intentional mentoring relationships. This is one of our sweetest joys in life and ministry.

In addition, mentoring can also be a spontaneous encounter in which a mentor provides insight and perspective to another that changes their life.

Definition of *Spontaneous Intentional Mentoring*: An unplanned encounter in which one offers preplanned advice or counsel—words that helps the recipient in their development.

Definition of *Spontaneous Unintentional Mentoring*: An unplanned encounter in which one shares something unknowingly that results in helpful advice, counsel, and encouragement.

	Spontaneous Intentional Mentoring	*Spontaneous Unintentional Mentoring*
Scheduled	No	No
Prepared to Share	Yes	No
Awareness of the Mentoring Moment	Yes	No

An example of mentoring is when an effective teacher, whom you deeply respect, cares for you at a sacrificial level, offering wisdom and advice that is relevant and helpful, whether planned or spontaneous.

I would like to encourage you again with the fact that some mentoring can happen unintentionally and spontaneously. This can happen in moments together when one gains life-changing perspective, knowledge, wisdom and/or help from another.

These are the unexpected times—a sudden phone call, an impromptu visit, or a casual unplanned encounter afford opportunities to speak into your protégé's life and vice versa. Often, it is the unexpected moment that God uses to touch a life in a very meaningful way. We have named these moments *spontaneous unintentional* or *intentional mentoring*. This displays the power of God working in a life, and we are simply the instruments that He uses to touch that heart and mind.

Frequently, we have heard people reference an encounter with us over lunch or over a weekend when this happened. We were totally unaware of the impact of that particular *spontaneous unintentional mentoring*.

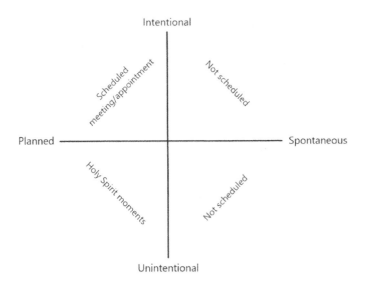

Here are nine questions that you should consider when thinking about mentoring.

Question 1: How does a mentoring relationship begin?

You may be wondering: does the mentor ask the protégé, or does the protégé ask the mentor? Most often, the mentor takes the first step in the relationship by offering to help a protégé to succeed. Because the mentor is committed to a lifetime of offering attention, encouragement and help, the mentor prayerfully seeks, chooses, and approaches a protégé. However, there are times when a protégé may need to approach a mentor. That was my experience years ago when Jorge Carvalho asked me if I would be willing to mentor him. God used that request to begin our journey of mentoring couples (see chapter 5).

The best advice is: don't wait for the ideal moment. If you are either a mentor or a protégé, and you are ready to seek someone out, go for it. As you approach that person, acknowledge that you have noticed them, and that God has singled them out to you. You can explain what you have been praying for and what you can envision having with him/her. A word of encouragement is "Initiate!" As a mentor or a protégé!

Pause here. Who comes to your mind at this moment when you think of mentoring someone? Or being mentored by someone?

Question 2: How much time does a mentoring relationship require?

Every mentoring relationship takes a different amount of time. In terms of frequency, it may involve connecting once a week, once or twice a month, or even quarterly. It could also be a week-end encounter. The amount of time that you invest will depend upon your relationship, the needs and circumstances. You may begin with an initial understanding of your time commitment and then allow it to change to give either more or less time. We normally meet at pre-set times— anywhere from 45-60 minutes to much longer.

The important thing to recognize here is that mentoring takes time. Occasionally it can be inconvenient or somewhat out of your comfort zone, but it is always well worth your time. You can always set a pre-determined trial period with your protégé to test out your experience together— perhaps meet two or three times to see how it goes.

In terms of the duration of your mentoring relationship, this too will depend upon your relationship, the needs and circumstances. Sometimes mentoring begins with a definite ending time in mind. At other times, the mentoring is continuous and ongoing. When a protégé's role or responsibilities change, this may cause a relationship to conclude. Always remain sensitive to the Holy Spirit's leading.

Question 3: What do we talk about when we meet?

It is often helpful to have several questions in mind when you begin a mentoring conversation, such as: "What has God done recently in your life that you are grateful for?" or "What is something that you have had to face recently that has been a challenge?" or "What would be a meaningful thing for us to focus on today?"

The protégé may be ready as well to share regarding:

- Pressing decisions they are facing

- Problems that are impeding life or ministry

- Plans that they have recently begun thinking about

- Progress that they have made since the last mentoring session

- Prayer requests

- Family, team or relational concerns

There are seven areas we desire to see developing in the lives of our protégés.

1. Family and Marriage

2. Finances

3. Personal Growth (educational, emotional, hobbies, etc.)

4. Physical (health, exercise, nutrition, etc.)

5. Professional/Ministerial

6. Social/cultural adaptation

7. Spiritual Life

You might consider encouraging your protégé to make a list of questions that he/she is trying to answer, ideally in order of priority. The more the protégé is prepared and ready to engage with their mentor, the more eager the mentor will be to teach and share their best. It works both ways.

One thing that my wife and I have always practiced as we prepare to mentor is PRAYER. We always pray before we begin a mentoring session. We also pray with our protégés as we finish; and after we finish, Laurie and I again thank the Lord for all that He did during our time together. This binds us together more strongly as mentor and protégé.

Question 4: What communication options facilitate our mentoring relationships?

One may assume that most mentoring is done face to face. For some, that is the most natural and realistic way. That has not been our practice. Many of the people that we are mentoring have lived far away from us in other countries (i.e. Brazil, Romania, Mozambique, Italy, India, China, Spain, Portugal, etc., to name a few).

For those who depend on technology, there are many programs that serve well: Skype, Zoom, WhatsApp, FaceTime, etc. One needs to know what is available for both the mentor and the protégé so that both can have the strongest connection and signal with the least interference. Sometimes, due to local conditions, and/or time zones, one must sacrifice their time of day or night to make the conversation possible.

For those who live in close proximity to one another, there are various possibilities: coffee shops, meeting rooms, someone's home, at church, etc.

Question 5: Should I ever tell my protégé what to do?

Be careful to build trust and be patient. As you continue to ask: "What are your priorities?" and "How can I help?" there will come a day when your protégé will turn to you and ask, "Well, what do you think?" At that point, you can definitely capitalize on the question and share your heart with them. They want to know what you think because they have come to trust you completely.

You should feel 100 percent free to express your concerns, share your excitement, tell them how you see the situation and let them respond. These contributions can help them see from a different perspective. Your insights can trigger further thoughts, and ideas and discovery. This very healthy dialogue can produce an even tighter bond between you and your protégé.

Question 6: What should I do if my protégé doesn't follow through with our original agreement?

First of all, stay positive. Assume the protégé wants to get together but is just busy or has a legitimate reason for not following through. Take the initiative. Don't let your fears or anxiety build. Don't automatically read rejection into a silence or a distance. Chances are about 99 percent that you are not being rejected.

You may need to review your agreement and reaffirm each person's commitment to it. Or you may need to redefine your relationship to require less time or agree to a meeting time or frequency that is better for both of your schedules. Don't give up; try to redefine before ending a mentoring relationship.

Question 7: If I have a genuine fear of being rejected in a mentoring relationship, how do I deal with it?

Personally, we have not experienced this fear, but we acknowledge that it could be an issue. Therefore, trust is the key.

First of all, it is ok to just spend time with a person in order to move the trust level higher and higher, so that you can formalize the relationship into one of mentoring. Make it a gradual process. If you are concerned about rejection, we would suggest that you need to wait to discuss this subject or mentoring and bring your fear to the Lord for His help first. Just relax, enjoy the relationship, build trust and grow together. After trust is built and you sense the prompting of the Holy Spirit, introduce the concept of a mentoring relationship. Also, emphasize that "fit" is a key, and that is not a negative thing; it is just a reality that some personalities fit together better than others.

Question 8: How do I get out of a mentoring relationship?

Getting out of a mentoring relationship is no different than getting out of any other kind of relationship. It is a personal and difficult issue to work through. There are three words that are key here: Care, Honest, and Fair. One can say, "I *care* far too much about you not to be *honest* with you. And in *fairness* to you, I think we need to slow down, stop, change or redefine our mentoring relationship." After that, one can explain further. Focus on positive learning that has taken place. Be direct in kindness regarding your reasons for stopping.

Question 9: Can I be a mentor if I have never had one?

Absolutely! You will find it harder if you have never had a mentor as a model, but it is not more difficult than being a good parent when you didn't have a "model" parent. If you have experience, encouragement to share, and desire to mentor, by all means do it.[1]

You might consider finding a mentor who would mentor you as you begin mentoring others. Chapter 11 will provide some insights into the kind of mentor to look for. A healthy relationship with a mentor will provide you a model and support and encouragement as you mentor.

Questions for Reflection...

1. As you think of mentoring, who comes to mind? Who is someone who you would like to mentor in the future?

2. What might be your next steps to take with that person or persons?

In 2009, my wife, Virginia, and I met the Keyes and our lives changed forever. God brought Bill and Laurie into our lives as mentors and has used them to challenge and inspire us to be better parents, spouses, and missionaries. What amazes us the most is that whenever we talk to them, even though they have a lot of experience, they always bring something fresh to the conversation from their devotional time that very morning.

For them, the most important thing is to "keep the main thing the main thing." What else should I say about them? They exceeded our expectations: "They gave themselves first of all to the Lord, and then by the will of God also to us" (2 Corinthians 8:5).

Jorge Carvalho
Friend, Pastor, Missionary
OC/Sepal Director in Romania

Chapter 9
Anyone Can Mentor but
Not Everyone Will

Yes, many people can become mentors, but not
everyone will mentor. This is not an excuse; not
everyone is prepared to mentor. If a person is strongly
egocentric, this person would need to become more
humble and teachable before mentoring others.
Another point mentioned earlier is that some are very
gifted and strongly given to other areas of ministry. We
each need to use the gifting that God has given to us,
and mentoring can always be an option. As you gain life
experience, you begin to discover how God has
equipped and gifted you. Be who God has blessed you
to be and consider mentoring according to your gifting.

You can be a mentor by helping someone who has a
desire to learn and a teachable spirit, but who has less
experience than you. A spiritually mature person can

mentor someone who is newer to faith, even if that person is much older (as illustrated by Laurie's protégé in Chapter 7).

A senior citizen can mentor a mature adult.

A mature adult can mentor a young adult.

A young adult can mentor a college student.

A college student can mentor a high school student.

A high school student can mentor someone in middle school.

And, of course, even a younger person can mentor someone older.

Anyone who really wants to can become a mentor.

I remember when I was in college, Jim Dwinell, my youth director, gave me the challenge of working with high schoolers in our church. It was that experience that caused me to refocus my personal goals as well as my academic studies. Instead of preparing for teaching in a secular high school, my new focus was ministry with youth, high school and college students. After my graduation from seminary, I became totally committed to working with young people in a training/mentoring role.

In the book *Mentoring*, Bobb Biehl writes about three different phases that a person can find themselves in. We have also experienced these phases.

1. The Survival Phase: This is when someone is in an extremely stressful period of life. Even the slightest additional commitment would put them under. This is not the time to consider mentoring. You need to have something extra in the tank to give to others if you are going to mentor.

2. The Success Phase: This is when someone is experiencing the "crest of the wave" with activity, success and accomplishment. It could be your company, your church, your school or family. The responsibilities are growing so quickly that you can hardly keep up. Like the first phase, this is not the best time to consider taking on another major commitment. You should wait to see that some of your areas of responsibility have either shifted, dropped or been accomplished before you consider mentoring. We must always be open to what God is doing in our lives, as He may be leading us to a different set of priorities.

3. The Significance Phase: This is when a person is at a point in their life where they are asking the question: "How can I really make a difference in someone's life?" They may have more time on their hands for one reason or another.[1]

Understanding these phases may help you discern your readiness to mentor others. There are two main factors that should be considered when you are thinking about mentoring. First, you may be involved in many activities, but you know that God is asking you to adjust your priorities, make time, and even be willing to sacrifice in obedience to His clear leading to mentor. Be sure you are hearing the Lord ask you to take this step of faith. Secondly, you may not have developed in life beyond a certain point, but you realize that God has given you something to pass on to others. God may be asking you to consider taking that step of faith. Give this some thought as you reflect on the phase that you most identify with.

Howard and William Hendricks, in their book *As Iron Sharpens Iron,* outline five benefits of being a mentor: "1) a close relationship with another [person], 2) personal renewal, 3) a sense of self-fulfillment, 4) enhanced self-esteem, and 5) an impact through your life."[2] Consider these gains as you evaluate your readiness to mentor.

Questions for Reflection...

1. In which of the three phases do you find yourself today?

2. How does this awareness affect your ability right now to mentor someone?

Chapter 10
What a Mentor Looks for in a Protégé

Protégés are individuals we are called to invest in. We literally give them part of our life, energy and experience. Here we have listed some qualities that a mentor looks for in a protégé.

Your Ideal Protégé is...

- Easy to believe in

- Easy to enjoy and spend time with naturally

- Easy to keep helping

- Someone who could become like family

- Ready to learn

- One who respects/admires you

- Self-motivated

- Truthful

- Comfortable spending time with you

- Someone with whom you can easily develop a relationship

- Responsible

- Dependable

- Someone who wants to grow[1]

Going back to my days in Brazil when I was ministering with the OC Sepal Brazil team, we used to say that we were looking for FAT people: Faithful, Available and Teachable. We still look for FAT people to mentor today.

It is important to note that generally, your future protégé wants you to mentor them as much as you want to mentor him or her. It needs to be a mutual desire and commitment.

Further considerations for selecting your first protégé:

First, make a list of all the people you could see as possible protégés. Then consider making a list of the top two or three. As you begin this selection process, consider their desire to be mentored, their availability, their readiness to be mentored and the evidences that they would respond well to you as a mentor.

Secondly, as a mentor, define what you purpose to give your protégé. This will be based upon what you see as their strengths, weaknesses, experiences, knowledge and passions.

Thirdly, consider your personal strengths and experiences in life. Reflect on how God has uniquely shaped you. What are your:

- Spiritual gifts

- Heart passions

- Abilities

- Personality

- Experiences

Fourthly, now look at your list of potential protégés to see who seems to match who God has made you to be. As this moment is so crucial, stop and ask the Lord to make this decision very clear to you and to your eventual choice.

Note: It is possible that you may want to have more than one protégé at the same time. Consider your available time and the Lord's leading in this decision. For years now, my wife and I have recognized a certain ability to keep life in balance when we limit ourselves to 12 couples or individuals at a time. After all, Jesus did it with 12, and perhaps for a good reason. All of our protégés have regular times with us. Our mentoring occupies nearly two-thirds of our ministry. We love mentoring all those that God gives us. At times, this also includes spontaneous and planned mentoring with some of our grandchildren.

What's next...?

Now it is time to approach your first candidate. As you contact this person, share how God has placed them on your heart. Share what you have been thinking and praying about. Explain what mentoring means to you. Give them some time to process this and listen carefully to how they respond. The bottom line is that you are offering something of yourself to help them to become the person that God desires them to be. You are not the only instrument that God is using or will use, but you are offering to make them a priority in your life to bring encouragement, relationship and counsel in many different forms.

In meeting with this person, each of you needs to know what to expect from the other. Here is a helpful list to consider discussing together.

- The frequency of your mentorship encounters

- What's expected in preparation, if anything

- The length of each meeting

- The location (if in person)

- Communication options (if not in person)

- The level of confidentiality

- The degree of commitment

These are the factors that need to be mutually understood and agreed to. Some of these factors may only become apparent as you start meeting together. Both of you need to sense that you are ready and willing to make this commitment to each other.[2]

Questions for Reflection...

1. As a mentor, when you look for a protégé, which of the mentioned qualities do you consider most important?

2. Reviewing the additional considerations for selecting a protégé, what are your thoughts?

3. If you have already started a mentoring relationship, how will you strengthen this relationship?

Chapter 11
What a Protégé Looks for in a Mentor

It is common in the beginning to have some fear about approaching someone to mentor you. You may be thinking, "Why would this person want to spend time with me? What would they find in me that would make them interested in spending time with me?"

To face this issue, it is helpful to move your thoughts away from yourself and to have in mind a clear idea of what you are looking for in a mentor. Here is a checklist to help you. Before you choose someone, look to see which of these qualities are evident.

Your ideal mentor is:

- Honest with you

- A model for you, especially in the areas that you want to grow

- Available

- Committed to you with a willingness to be there for you

- Open and transparent with you

- A teacher/clear communicator

- One who believes in your potential

- One who can help you define your direction and make a plan with you.

- A good model

- Willing to stay primarily on your agenda, not her/his own

- Open to learning from you, as well as to teaching you[1]

If you don't find a good number of these qualities in the person you are considering, there is a strong possibility that the mentoring relationship may be less than satisfying to both of you.

In their book *TransforMissional Coaching,* Steve Ogne and Tim Roehl talk about four character traits that are essential for good coaches (and likewise good mentors) to have. They should be: 1) Spiritually active, 2) Personally secure, 3) Growing both personally and professionally, and 4) Have integrity in relationships.[2] If the person you are choosing to be your mentor has these four qualities, there is a high likelihood that the relationship will be mutually satisfying.

What a Protégé Looks for in a Mentor

Once you know what you are looking for in a mentor, here are steps for selecting and approaching a potential mentor.

- Define what you need and/or want from a mentor.

- Make a list of 2 or 3 potential mentor candidates.

- Compare the ideal mentor checklist (above) to these candidates.

- Review these insights into mentoring to see whom of your potential mentors fits best.

  "Mentoring is a lifelong relationship in which a mentor helps a protégé reach his or her God-given potential." – Bobb Biehl

  "In addition, mentoring can also be a spontaneous encounter in which a mentor provides insight and perspective to another that changes their life." – Bill Keyes

- Ask God to make it clear to you.

- Meet with the person to share your desire to be mentored by them—clarifying the results you desire from a mentoring relationship

- Once you both agree, be fully committed to the relationship and the process.

Make certain that both of you have the same expectations. In addition to the list at the end of the previous chapter, here are some areas to consider and discuss together:

- What are the specific needs the protégé feels at the moment?

- Ideally, how long do we expect the relationship to last?

- Are there any limits we want to establish?

- Are there any issues that may have caused previous mentoring relationships to be disappointing that would be wise to discuss at the beginning?

- What are our expectations?

- What anxieties, uncertainties, uneasiness and inadequacies, if any, do we feel about this relationship?

Caution: Don't overcommit at the beginning. Work it out as you go. You may want to discuss these matters again after a pre-determined period of time. You might simply say, "Let's commit to this for eight weeks and then evaluate how it is going."

Questions for Reflection...

1. As a protégé, or someone who desires to be one, how do you measure yourself with the list of qualities noted in chapter 10, those of an ideal protégé?

2. As a protégé, how do you assess either the person you wish to mentor you, or the person you have already chosen?

3. What are you asking God to do in order to make your relationship stronger?

Some years ago, I was at Aguas de Lindoia participating in a Sepal training program for new missionaries in Brazil. Early one morning, before breakfast, I put on my tennis shoes and sport clothes to go outside for some exercise. The morning was beautiful. There were flowers and trees everywhere, a small lake, different types of birds... and who did I see there getting their morning exercise? Bill, our friend and example.

He has been an example in so many ways. Although he comes from a different culture then mine, he always appreciates Brazilians. Reflecting on our conversations, mentoring times, travels together, discussions around the dinner table, talking on Skype—the person I see is a faithful servant of Christ who each day wants to be more like Christ.

In his mentoring, it is not his teaching that impacts as much as what he lives and is passionate about. This is Bill: mentor, friend, example, good conversationalist and funny. We have spent a lot of time together. At one point, I had the courage to ask Laurie, "Is Bill always happy and joyful or are there times when he is down at some point in the day?" Laurie smiled and said, "He is always that happy and joyful."

Perfect? Certainly not! I can only remember seeing Bill really tired two times in all our many years of journeying together. Most of my encounters have shown him to be an energetic, joyful servant with the disposition to help others, offering wise counsel with a smile. Bill is a great friend who follows Christ.

Sirley Prado
*Friend, Missionary/Director of personnel Sepal/ Brazil
Clinical psychologist*

Chapter 12
How to be a Good Mentor

During my days in seminary, one of my favorite professors, Dr. Bill Bynum, showed a particular interest in me. He affirmed me as a person and gave me a vision for what I could become in the field of Christian Education. He motivated me to aspire to a level beyond what I was seeing for myself at that time. He believed in me and affirmed me as someone who could achieve what I set out to do. That was a great motivation at that stage in my life, and a powerful example of good mentoring.

Later on, while serving as Director of Personnel and giving myself fully to recruitment, training and caring for our missionaries in OC International, I experienced *spontaneous intentional mentoring* in my life. One day, Rev. Paul Yaggy, who was interim President for OCI, came to me in the lunchroom, placed his hand on my shoulder and said, "Bill, you are one of the best recruiters in missions." Whether that was true or not, he affirmed me that day in what I was giving a lot of energy to, and it made a difference. He was used by God to motivate me in a deep way with both the physical touch on my shoulder and affirming words of value. He met with me regularly and I always anticipated those special times with him. He was a great mentor to me. He would ask me how I was doing, probe what I was struggling with and listen as I shared what I was hearing from God. Anticipating this always kept me on the alert to these issues.

Paul Yaggy challenged me to be a leader. Over time, I have appreciated Paul Hersey's definition of leadership. "Leadership is any attempt to influence the behavior of another individual or group."[1] Leadership refers to relationships in which you are working with others with the purpose of seeing them achieve their God-given potential.

The focus of "heart to heart" is more important than "head to head." I felt the hearts of these men louder than their words, and yet their words were life-changing because of their hearts for me.

We resonate with the five important elements that Bobb Biehl identified for being a good mentor. We have fleshed them out over years of mentoring relationships. We strongly urge you to embrace these five non-negotiables for effective mentoring:

1. Love: Love your protégé. This is the key to a meaningful relationship. When your protégé sees, feels and knows real love from you, that is the strongest bridge for building into a life. That attitude of love can dispel fear, doubt and even a certain resistance to being mentored. Pray for a positive initial impression that God can use to build the foundation of your relationship. It is also important that you express love with care and gentleness. We all need to hear that we are loved and valued from time to time. In addition, sometimes it is necessary to care enough to confront in love. This relationship can offer that opportunity as long as it is genuine and sincere.

2. Encourage: We all need to be encouraged, affirmed and recognized for what we do. The comment, "I'm on your team and we will do it together" can go miles at a crucial moment in a person's life. Telling someone that they will make it is so important. Reflect on the potential that you see in your protégé and affirm them in specific areas, such as speaking, good leadership, evangelism, teaching, music, being friendly, being a strong team player, etc.

3. Be open: Model transparency. One of the best ways a protégé learns is from your own experiences as you share your failures as well as your successes. One key lesson that we learned from the founder of our mission, Dr. Dick Hillis, is, "It is not wrong to fail, as long as we learn from our failures." Sharing your failures and what you have learned from them is vital to your protégé's growth as well. We all need to be open, realistic and truthful. The mentor is modeling here in a quiet but powerful way.

4. Check your motives: Your purpose and motive in mentoring is never to upstage your protégé, but rather to support them and stay committed to their needs and agenda. You want to make your protégé look and feel as good as you possibly can with the right motives and efforts. Honoring them, thanking them, and recognizing positive things about them, when said truthfully, can really build stronger relationships. You will know if you are doing this well by how they respond to you.

Good leaders are willing to serve. The true mentor serves people. Serving means not always doing what is most popular but doing what is best for your protégé. "True leaders are motivated by loving concern rather than a desire for personal glory."[2] This must be our motivation as we mentor.

5. Relax: Normally, as a mentor, you are older than the protégé, but not always. In either case, if the protégé wants to learn from the mentor, there needs to be a mutual ability to be relaxed and comfortable in the relationship. A strong relationship is built when you as a mentor love, care, relax, and see what God is doing in your protégé's life. A key to this is genuine affirmation. Enjoy them.[3]

Brent Eldridge observes, "Like automobiles, human beings need gas station experiences. We need to be filled up in order to keep moving down Productivity Lane."[4] The best mentors are the ones that have cultivated a relationship of encouragement where each time they meet with their protégé, the protégé is revitalized to do what it is that they discover to be their action plan.

Questions for Reflection...

1. In this chapter, the focus was on being an effective mentor, focusing on five non-negotiables. In which areas are you the strongest? In which areas are you weaker?

2. What would you ask God for in order to be a stronger mentor?

For us, as a Brazilian missionary couple and family serving in Italy, it has been a joy these past years to be mentored by Bill and Laurie. Without a doubt, we have felt God's love for us through their friendship, concern and care for us. It is so refreshing to have a mature, older couple with wonderful insight offer experienced counsel and pray for us. Their experiences as a couple, as parents and as missionaries are God's gift to us. Most of all, they have helped us remember who God is and what He has done and is doing in our lives.

To have a mentorship focused on God, where the concern is how we are doing and not only what we are doing, enables us to do what He wants. Their concern is with our personal lives first, then as a couple and also as parents. During this journey, they have shared many challenges with us; we cry, pray and watch God work in our lives. We thank the Lord together for all of this. We thank God for Bill and Laurie's lives and for their example.

Luiz and Sara Santos
Friends, Missionaries with Sepal/Brazil, serving in Italy

Chapter 13
Mentoring Couple to Couple

The method of "mentoring couple to couple" has been a gift to us. It was a surprise blessing that God gave us— the privilege of mentoring another couple who desires to grow and learn from us. In recent years, my wife and I have enjoyed this immensely. We typically mentor missionary couples and some pastoral couples. We find it to be a natural way to connect with both husband and wife. It has proved to be very beneficial and effective for various reasons.

Often, a man can speak to a man and a woman can speak to a woman more effectively. This happens even when couples work with couples. Also, when a couple works together, they have combined gifts, insights and a fuller perspective as a unit that can be offered to the protégé couple. The bonding is just as strong or may be even stronger than in one-on-one mentoring, as there is greater accountability when you work together as a foursome.

There is a special joy and togetherness that a couple feels when they serve together. It strengthens their relationship. This is also true for the protégé couple as they are processing and learning together, and then applying and living what they've learned together.

Mentoring as a couple is a strong model for other couples. A couple's relationship is enriched when they see how they can work together, even when their personal ministries differ. Often a man has his ministry and a woman has hers, and by experiencing mentorship together, their lives are brought closer. They have more to share and discuss together. This can even lead to further potential ministry to other couples.

In our role as missionaries, many of those that we serve are couples. They seem to enjoy being mentored together for the intrinsic value it has for their marriage. Pastors are not often with their wives in ministry and mentoring them as a couple is an abundantly rich experience. Working together on marriage, family and ministry issues brings a natural strengthening factor to the marriage. Couples in secular work experience the same benefit.

Think about those that are serving within your sphere of influence. Who do you see that could be challenged and encouraged to accept this particular kind of mentorship couple to couple?

Questions for Reflection...

1. (For married couples) Have you ever experienced couple mentoring, either as a protégé or a mentor? In what ways did you find it helpful?

2. How open is your spouse to this experience?

3. What couple could you mentor? What couple could mentor you?

Chapter 14
Mentoring in a Group
My Personal Story

By Laurie Keyes

Years ago, I received a letter from our oldest daughter, Donna, who was overwhelmed as a young mom. She was intent on encouraging me as an "empty nester" to make myself available to younger women in response to a society with few older women with a vision and heart to mentor.

Shortly after reading her letter to me, the most important letter in the world had an even deeper impact on my life—it was God's letter. As I read Titus 2, parts of phrases stood out to me: "teach the older women... to be an example in the way they live... to teach what is good... then they can train the younger women... to love their husband and their children... to be self-controlled and pure... to be keepers at home."

These phrases challenged me to begin thinking about the importance of spending time mentoring young women. These two letters fueled my desire to be available as a "mentor mom."

My personal journey into group mentoring began when three young women came to me for mentoring all within a week. I told each one that I would love to have that privilege, but that I needed to pray and check my calendar. I asked each of them to do the same. It soon became apparent to me that three separate mentoring encounters were not possible given the commitments I already had. We decided to wait for summer to pass and then meet together at my home to discuss our schedules. By the time we got together at the end of summer, each of them had three friends who also wanted mentoring relationships. I opened the door to my home and there stood twelve very excited young women with the desire to be mentored.

I remember saying to them as we began, "Well, Jesus did it with twelve. Perhaps that is what we could try. Perhaps a group mentoring experience could work." We met together weekly for twelve weeks and discovered a very powerful mentoring tool! I was the older women mentoring young moms who in turn were mentoring one another in various aspects of just living life joyfully.

I developed subjects we could talk about, thinking of their roles in five areas of life: 1) woman, 2) wife, 3) mom, 4) child of God and 5) servant in the church, community and the world. Because I believe that the Bible is very relevant to the world we live in today, all the subjects that we talked about had a basis in the Bible. We provided each mom with a worksheet that included a "hook paragraph" to introduce them to the subject of the week and a few verses for them to consider individually. (See Appendix for sample studies.)

After four months, many of their friends were asking for this mentoring experience as well. We let it grow, not wanting to be exclusive. When 30 women signed up, I knew I would need to recruit two older women to join me who could each take on ten. The women I approached were women I knew could do it. However, because they had never mentored before, they were very hesitant. I was able to encourage them with the thought that I would be sharing the main thoughts each week, then each of us would simply take a group of ten into a different part of the house to discuss and pray together about that day's topic.

It worked beautifully; and it even evoked in these mentor moms the desire to speak on each topic because they had their own personal thoughts to contribute. I discovered that God had arranged an experience for me that was in direct obedience to Titus 2:3, "teach the older women" and 2:4, "... then they can train the younger women." Amazing!

The next time we had the same opportunity (which was after the summer break), we had 120 sign up to be with us. Each of the older women took on some of the main subjects we chose to address. That is mentoring! As has been mentioned already in this book, mentoring is not a program; it is "life on life" based one's own experience in life, not based on a curriculum or program.

Because our group had grown so large, we decided to recruit seven other mentors, and changed our location. I was able to share during the main mentoring time with the larger group of moms, then we broke into ten separate spaces for further mentoring on the subject presented, in groups of 10-12 women each. The dynamic we all enjoyed together was unstoppable.

Starting with the first three moms in 1995, we grew to 120 moms and called ourselves "Moms & Beyond." By 1998 there were already other churches asking us about "group mentoring experience" and they began doing the same. Once again, God was leading me to live out what He had called us to in the very beginning of our ministry life, the multiplication process we see modeled in II Timothy 2:2, "... *and what you have heard from me in the presence of many witnesses, entrust to faithful men who will be able to teach others also."* (ESV)

To God be the glory. To this day, I still hear from many of those women who are now experiencing "empty nests" and have become "the older women"/ "the Mentor Moms" (as we were called back in the day). Now over 20 years have gone by and they too have started groups of their own.

I believe that I was given the gift of literally watching God do through us Ephesians 3:20, "*Now to Him who is able to do far more abundantly than all that we ask or think..."* (ESV) He took the need of those first few women who desired to have a mentor in their lives and He grew something we never even thought about or asked for! I recognize that this whole mentoring experience was totally of God.

One other mentoring opportunity developed out of this experience. They say that "necessity is the mother of invention." We developed a mentoring group for our

"Mentor Moms," coming out of their personal need for brain storming and prayer for their groups. This became a time for their encouragement, discussion of issues that surfaced in their group discussions, and prayer together. During this time, the "Mentor Moms" themselves were being mentored. The older women were becoming aware of the wonderful opportunity mentoring could be. Very few had ever been mentored themselves.

One more thought that I would like to encourage moms who are reading this book with: Take the challenge. Start a group mentoring experience. Take Titus 2:3-4 seriously, "Teach the older women." (NIV) Recruit some older women that you respect and cast the vision of mentoring younger women. I did this with a lovely coffee/tea by invitation.

Think of topics that you wish someone had mentored you in related to your role as a woman, wife, mom, and one who cares about her community. Launch a group mentoring experience that enables moms to be mentored and grow together.

(Note: The Appendix includes more information about Moms & Beyond, as well as some sample studies. You can also download this information at courseofamentor.com.)

Questions for Reflection...

1. After reading Laurie's story, what thoughts come to your mind regarding group mentoring?

2. If this is a possibility for you, what might be your plan of action?

Part 3
Pressing On

FINISH

My Nana and Papa are the two most intentional people I know. It is not uncommon for them to sit down with me and open our conversation with, "Okay, let's just get straight into it. How is your heart doing?" Their questions involve the details of my life that I have previously shared, details they have remembered and prayed over since our last time together. Because of geographical distance, our one-on-ones are limited to a couple times a year, but they are always rich with intentional sharing, encouragement, and refreshment for my soul.

One of the most powerful aspects of their mentorship has been hearing them each share what they call "faith stones"—the pivotal moments in their lives that have shaped their walk with God and demonstrated His provision. I've benefitted from these stories in more ways than one. First, I get to know them as imperfect people as they share about times of fear, suffering, and doubt. I feel known in our common humanity. Secondly, I get to learn about God's provision and radical love through their lived experiences. Lastly, I have started recording my own "faith stones" and find myself returning to them for fresh faith in hard seasons.

It can be challenging to share the vulnerable details of our lives with others. There is relational work to be put in before it feels safe. My Nana and Papa's consistency in doing this kind of relational work over the course of my life has built a trust that makes it easy to share and to pick up right where we left off.

Anne Brady
Granddaughter of Bill and Laurie

Chapter 15
Mentoring the Next Generation of Mentors

Mentoring is a basic element in developing Christian leaders. A good definition of Christian leadership is: "Leadership is knowing what to do next, knowing why that's important, and knowing how to bring the appropriate resources to bear on the need at hand."[1] There are two forces at work at the same time: 1) The work of the Holy Spirit giving insight, understanding and conviction regarding the issue at hand. 2) The work of the mentor facilitating, guiding and encouraging the protégé to act upon what they discover within their mind and heart.

Dr. Dick Hillis told us years ago that the symbol of a good mentor/servant is a towel. It was Jesus who set the model. "Jesus picked up a towel and washed the feet of His disciples. He came to serve and to minister. We must do as He did, be servants to the whole body of Christ."[2]

One of the most exciting aspects of mentoring is when the protégé discovers for themselves what it is that God is saying to them individually. At that point, acknowledge that they have the privilege and opportunity to respond to what God is guiding them to do personally. These insights are the fruit of mentoring relationships.

Our challenge is to see discovery happen in as many lives as God enables us to touch, and through them to others, and through them to others, to at least the fourth generation. Again, reflecting on 2 Timothy 2, we see the Principle of Multiplication. Paul taught (and mentored) Timothy, and in return, Timothy taught (and mentored) faithful men who also trained (and mentored) others. There is a four generational impact here—Paul, Timothy, faithful men, others.

We obviously desire to help the person we are mentoring. At the same time, we are modeling and challenging our protégé in the discipline of mentoring

> Imagine this: If you were to mentor 12 people in your lifetime who each mentor 12 more, that equals 144... who mentor 12 more, equaling 1,728... who mentor 12 more, equaling 20,736... who mentor 12 more, equaling 248,832... who mentor 12 more, equaling 2,985,984! That's absolutely astounding! All this in just six generations of multiplication. You could impact nearly three million people in your lifetime if this just kept going.

others. Then, as they begin to mentor others, their mentoring relationship includes this "multiplication" dimension of challenging their protégé to mentor others in the fourth generation, and so on as God blesses.

This is an amazing picture of the multiplication process; look at the power of our part and what we could be contributing to. It all depends upon each person's dedication and faithfulness to the commitment of mentoring in partnership with the Holy Spirit.

Since 2010, Laurie and I have had the privilege of mentoring many of Sepal Brazil's cross-cultural missionaries, a number of independent missionary couples, and some pastors and their wives. We have mentored approximately 40 missionaries serving in 8 countries and God continues to add to that number. Mentoring these missionaries has been one of the most gratifying and rewarding ministries we have had.

"Perhaps the most strategic and fruitful work of modern missionaries is to help leaders of tomorrow develop their spiritual potential. This task requires careful thought, wise planning, endless patience, and genuine Christian love. It cannot be haphazard or ill-conceived."[3] *(J. Oswald Sanders)*

As the number of missionaries sent by Sepal Brazil increases, we recognize that we are not able to mentor all of them, nor have we tried. Multiplication is key. As Kubicek and Cockram put it in their book *The 100x Leader,* "Multiplication is the intentional transfer of knowledge, skills, and expertise into the lives of the people you lead," or in this case *mentor.*[4] A few years ago, we began encouraging those we are mentoring to multiply their experience with us into the lives of new missionaries that are entering the mission field.

It is our prayer that the multiplication factor continues onward. Many of them have begun mentoring the new Brazilian missionaries who are leaving Brazil to serve globally. We are now mentoring them to mentor others.

As we finish writing this book, we will be part of the third bi-annual Brazilian Sepal cross-cultural missionary retreat in Portugal. Many whom we mentor will be coming to this event. We will have the joy of seeing face-to-face those we mentor, and others that they are mentoring—that third generation. We rejoice at how God uses all of us to expand His Church. To Him be the glory.

Questions for Reflection...

1. Reflect on the principle of II Timothy 2:2 and the concept of multiplication.

2. As you mentor someone, how are you passing on to them the idea of reproducing what they are learning to someone else?

3. Reflect on how God is or could be using you in this way.

We sat at a table outside the coffee shop, hand in hand, as I poured my heart out—expressing the great disappointment and grief I had repressed for months. Compassion was written all over my Papa's face when he lovingly responded, 'Shannon, I understand how you feel.' I remember driving back home from that morning feeling deeply comforted and assured that I had a team fighting for me. Together Nana and Papa have loved me with a kind of strength that can only come from God. I am convinced He gave them to me not only to carry me through the hardest, most defining times of my life, but to stir me on in my faith; to call me higher.

Simply knowing I have people cheering me on, praying on my behalf, is empowering. Their encouragement and deep understanding of God's ways helps me brave the fiercest storms. What's great about mentorship is that learning from their lives has shaped how I choose to live my own. They have pioneered the things I have yet to face, and it gives me courage to know I have them as guides. I am grateful to be loved and led by them!

Shannon
Granddaughter of Bill and Laurie

Chapter 16
Where Do We Go from Here?

There is a phrase that has made an impact upon my life: "Every generation needs to discover for itself what God wants of them"—the truths, the values and the meaning of life. Truth is eternal. God's plan for humans never changes. Yet, we as human beings need to discover what that means to us personally. Mentoring is key to discovering this.

Relationships are central to good mentoring. As your protégés begin mentoring others, you will experience a unique synergy with them that is both motivating and energizing. When a protégé individually commits to be a mentor, the next generation continues on with what the previous generation has learned. As each generation continues to grow and learn, more is passed on to the one God has given them to mentor. Your decision today to multiply generations of mentors will determine what you do tomorrow and so it goes, generation after generation.

Have you given thought to what your legacy will be? Have you considered what you want to leave behind in the lives of others? Today is the beginning of the rest of your life. Paul's says in II Timothy 4:7, "*I have fought the good fight, I have finished the race, I have kept the faith.*" (ESV) Let's commit ourselves to running our race well, committed to finish the course and pursue "the crown of righteousness which the Lord, the righteous judge, will award to us on that day."

"The mentor also benefits a great deal from the mentoring relationship. If you involve yourself as a mentor, thirty years from now as you look back on your life, you will find that managing people is where you have gotten your feelings of *success*, and mentoring people is where you have gotten your feelings of *significance* and *satisfaction*."[1]

Yes, it is time to act! Join us on this journey. Let us impact our present generation, then the next, and those to follow them with our commitment to Mentoring and Multiplication.

Be a lifelong mentor.

Develop relationships that help you grow into your God-given potential and then help your protégés grow into their God-given potential. Learn to pass it on in such a way that they are inspired to pass it on—in such a way that they inspire others to pass it on again.

When we mentor, there are no guarantees regarding the outcome. We may not directly see or know the impact of our mentoring relationship. Yet, one day in heaven, for those who know Christ personally, we will really see and know the impact of our lives!

Oh, we pray that God says to all of us, "Well done, you good and faithful servant. Enter into your rest."

Question for Reflection...

Consider your sphere of influence, your field assigned by God (II Corinthians 10:13 and Psalm 16:5-6). My prayer is that your "field," your God-given purpose, is now further defined and apparent so as to multiply your life into the lives of many. How will you impact this "field" through mentoring relationships?

Share your mentoring journey with us at courseofamentor.com.

Final Challenge

Write out the action plan that you hear God asking you to develop. You are His instrument to further equip others with that which you have received.

Luke 12:48b "Everyone to whom much was given, of him much will be required." (ESV)

May God bless you as you move forward in faith and service.

Appendix

Moms & Beyond
A Mentoring Experience

The following pages describe some of the topics and studies used in the Moms & Beyond ministry (referenced in Chapter 14).

Teaching Topic Ideas

1. Role as a Woman

- Stages of a woman's life
- The friendships of women
- Caring for your body
- Watching your words
- Learning to listen
- Keeping your life balanced

2. Role as a Wife

- Seasons of marriage
- Love languages
- How males and females differ
- Being a helper/completer

- Communication/conflict resolution
- Importance of your sexual relationship

3. Role as a Mother

- Children—God's gift
- Learning to let go
- Discipline
- Each child is unique
- Practical parenting skills
- Playing with your child

4. Role as a Homemaker

- How to enjoy being a hostess
- Time management
- Money management
- Organizational skills
- Creating a warm atmosphere

5. Role in Your Community

- Friendship evangelism ideas
- Serving your neighbors
- Being salt and light
- Reaching the hurting

6. Role as a Child of God

- An adopted child of God

- Abiding in the Vine

- The Spirit-filled life

- Enriching your personal devotions

- Keeping a balanced life

- Prayer and spiritual warfare

- Holiness in an unholy world

- Forgiveness

- Commitment to the local church

Sample Study 1: An Adopted Child of God

Role as a Child of God

I will not leave you as orphans. I will come to you.
~ Jesus (John 14:18)

"From where did my feelings of alienation from God come? They did not appear overnight, but instead were the result of many years of being exposed to messages of condemnation and guild. No one had ever fully explained to me the core concept of the Christian faith, the message that God loves us, searches after us, and longs for us to be whole. I heard bits and pieces of this gospel, but never enough to fill my heart. In its absence I created my own theology, a patchwork quilt made up of false images of God."

~ James Bryan Smith, *Embracing the Love of God*

Verses to Read:

- John 3:16, 17

- 2 Peter 1:3

- Ephesians 1:19,20

- Galatians 5:22

Scripture to Memorize:

John 14:18

Questions to Contemplate:

1. What was Jesus' most singular purpose in coming to Earth?

2. What does that mean for you?

3. Have you truly experienced God's love in your life? Explain.

Sample Study 2: Seasons of Marriage

Role as a Wife

You and your spouse are artists bringing to the canvas of each other's life the potential that God has placed there.
~ H. Norman Wright (Quiet Times for Couples)

"God's intention is for our spouses to be our allies—intimate friends, lovers, warriors in the spiritual war against the forces of the evil one. We are to draw strength, nourishment, and courage to fight well from that one person who most deeply supports and joins us in the war—our soul mate. Husbands and wives are intimate allies."

~ Dan Allender & Tremper Longman, *Intimate Allies*

Appendix

Verses to Read:

Philippians 2:3,4

Philippians 2:13

Ephesians 5:1

Ephesians 5:21-22

Ephesians 5:25, 33

Questions to Contemplate:

1. What prevents you from seeing your husband as your ally in the storms of life?

2. What about your husband makes you grateful? How is he like Christ? How has his place in your life made you better?

Sample Study 3: Learning to Let Go

Role as a Mother

A parent must respect the spiritual person of his child, and approach it with reverence.
~ George H. MacDonald

"Being a mother is a lot like teaching a child to ride a bicycle. You have to know when to hold on and when to let go. If you lack this courage to let go, you'll get very tired of running along beside."

~ McConnell, *Thoughts on Motherhood*

Verses to Read:

Proverbs 3:5, 6

Hebrews 11:1

Romans 15:13

Matthew 11:28, 29

Luke 2:52

Questions to Contemplate:

1. How can you encourage and reward the growing independence of your child(ren)?

2. As the individuality of your child(ren) presents itself, what will keep you from trying to control and manipulate the personality to suit yourself? It is your God-give responsibility to shape the character of the child, but what is your response to the "personhood" of your child?

Notes

Chapter 6

1. Maxwell, John, *The 21 Most Powerful Minutes in a Leader's Day* (Thomas Nelson), 27.

Chapter 7

1. Biehl, Bobb, *Mentoring: Confidence in Finding a Mentor and Becoming One* (Nashville: Broadman & Holman Publishers, 1996), 29-30.

2. Ibid, 39-43.

Chapter 8

1. Biehl, Bobb, *Mentoring: Confidence in Finding a Mentor and Becoming One* (Nashville: Broadman & Holman Publishers, 1996), 44-57.

Chapter 9

1. Biehl, Bobb, *Mentoring: Confidence in Finding a Mentor and Becoming One* (Nashville: Broadman & Holman Publishers, 1996), 62-63.

2. Hendricks, Howard and William, *As Iron Sharpens Iron: Building Character in a Mentoring Relationship* (Chicago: Moody Press, 1995), 146.

Chapter 10

1. Biehl, Bobb, *Mentoring: Confidence in Finding a Mentor and Becoming One* (Nashville: Broadman & Holman Publishers, 1996), 126-129.

2. Ibid, 131-134.

Chapter 11

1. Biehl, Bobb, *Mentoring: Confidence in Finding a Mentor and Becoming One* (Nashville: Broadman & Holman Publishers, 1996), 104-108.

2. Ogne, Steve and Tim Roehl, *TransforMissional Coaching: Empowering Leaders in a Changing Ministry World* (Missional Challenge Publishing, 2019), 265-266.

Chapter 12

1. Hersey, Paul, *The Situational Leader* (Escondido: Center for Leadership Studies, 1984), 16.

2. White, John, *Excellence in Leadership: Reaching Goals with Prayer, Courage & Determination* (Madison, InterVarsity Press, 1986), 88.

3. Biehl, Bobb, *Mentoring: Confidence in Finding a Mentor and Becoming One* (Nashville: Broadman & Holman Publishers, 1996), 136-138.

4. Eldridge, Brent, *Team: Six Essentials for Building a Productive Team* (Eugene: Resource Publications), 53.

Chapter 15

1. Biehl, Bobb, *Leading with Confidence: Practical wisdom on leadership, management, and life* (Christian Art Publishers, 2010), 151.

2. Winebrenner, Jan, *Steel in His Soul: The Dick Hillis Story* (Mulkilteo, WinePress Publishing, 1996), 277.

3. Sanders, J. Oswald, *Spiritual Leadership* (Moody Publishers, 2017), 148.

4. Kubicek, Jeremie and Steve Cockram, *The 100x Leader: How to Become Someone Worth Following* (Hoboken: John Wiley & Sons, 2019), 136.

Chapter 16

1. Biehl, Bobb, *Mentoring: Confidence in Finding a Mentor and Becoming One* (Nashville: Broadman & Holman Publishers, 1996), 123.

Acknowledgments

Thanks...

To Bobb Biehl for authoring the book *Mentoring: Confidence in Finding a Mentor and Becoming One* that inspired me in the writing of my book. I am deeply grateful for his encouragement and mentoring.

To Dr. David DeVries, my son-in-law, a model spirit-driven leader, fellow missionary, founder and director of Missional Challenge, and MCWR Regional Director, for encouraging me to write and coaching me through the process.

To Janae Dueck, our granddaughter, for her skill and artwork that is represented inside the book.

To One Challenge International, for their support of us these 50 plus years of missionary service.

To Sepal Brazil where we served from 1967-1979, and with whom we continue to serve as volunteers globally.

To Missional Challenge for publishing the book.

To Rachael Grotte, who edited this book as a member of Missional Challenge and inspired us to write with clarity and integrity.

About the Authors

Bill and Laurie Keyes saw each other for the first time as nine-year-olds when their respective families first visited Fountain Avenue Baptist Church in Hollywood, CA. They were both raised in the Hollywood area by Christian parents and attended the same Christian High School, Culter Academy, in Los Angeles (now Linfield School in Temecula, CA).

After high school, Laurie studied at Biola College in La Mirada, CA, where she majored in Christian Education. Bill studied at Westmont College in Santa Barbara, CA, and continued his theological training at Talbot Theological Seminary receiving his Master's in Religious Education (MRE).

After graduation, they married and prepared for youth ministry in the USA; however, God redirected them into foreign missions. They joined Overseas Crusades (today One Challenge International). After two years of Missionary Internship in Pontiac, MI, and support raising, they left for Brazil to join the OC Brazil team in 1967 with a 3-year-old, Donna, a 2-year-old, Deanne, and a 3-month-old, Darlene. Their son, Dale, was born during their first term of service.

Bill and Laurie served in Brazil for 13 years. They founded the organization Association of Christian Education (ALEC). Over the years, more than 14,000 pastors, leaders and Sunday school teachers were trained. In addition, Bill served as the field director for Sepal/Brazil for four years. Today it is fully led by Brazilians. In 1979, they returned home for furlough. The mission asked them to stay home to take over the leadership of the Recruitment Department for OCI.

Bill served for 30 years as Vice President of Personnel, responsible for recruitment, pre-field training (including MKs), member-care, church relations and leadership development. Laurie was a large part of all this ministry as well. They both served in leadership positions at their home church in Colorado Springs as well. During these years, Laurie was held at gunpoint as a hostage with three others at Focus on the Family. Many passages of Scripture, God's presence and His rescue again proved His faithfulness in deep and abiding ways.

In 2010, they returned to Brazil at the invitation of the Brazil team to help them develop a Personnel Department that recruits, trains, and supports sending missionaries cross-culturally. After six months there, they returned to the USA to take on a mentoring role, caring for all cross-cultural missionaries sent out of Brazil.

Bill and Laurie currently live in Bellevue, Washington, and are active in their local church. They continue their missionary ministry mentoring and encouraging those they are committed to as the Lord leads.

For over 53 years, they have ministered to hundreds of missionaries, pastors, and church leaders. The heart of their ministry is mentorship—a relational ministry that extends to each and every person that they serve.

About the Authors

Together, their life verse is Psalm 34:3, "Oh magnify the Lord with me, and let us exalt His name together."

Made in the USA
Monee, IL
02 November 2023

45620837R00083